CHILDREN IN CHAOS

CHILDREN IN CHAOS

*How Israel and the United States
Attempt to Integrate At-Risk Youth*

IVAN C. FRANK

Westport, Connecticut
London

Library of Congress Cataloging-in-Publication Data

Frank, Ivan Cecil.
   Children in chaos : how Israel and the Untied States attempt to
integrate at-risk youth / Ivan C. Frank.
      p.   cm.
   Includes bibliographical references and index.
   ISBN 0-275-94291-0 (alk. paper)
      1. Socially handicapped youth—Services for—Israel.   2. Socially
handicapped youth—Services for—United States.   I. Title.
HV1441.I8F73   1992
362.7'4—dc20   92-7484

British Library Cataloguing in Publication Data is available.

Library of Congress Catalog Card Number: 92-7484
ISBN: 0-275-94291-0

First published in 1992

Praeger Publishers, 88 Post Road West, Westport, CT 06881
An imprint of Greenwood Publishing Group, Inc.

Printed in the United States of America

The paper used in this book complies with the
Permanent Paper Standard issued by the National
Information Standards Organization (Z39.48-1984).

10 9 8 7 6 5 4 3 2 1

This book, <u>Children in Chaos</u>, is dedicated to our children, Ayal and Michal—two young people who are sensitive to youth raised under much more difficult circumstances than they were.

Contents

List of Tables.. ix

Preface.. xi

Introduction 1

1. Changing Youths' Attitudes: Well-meaning Attempts in the
   United States 7
2. Warehousing Our Children: Another Dismal Failure......................... 15
3. Some Good Educational Programs: A Brief Overview......................... 21
4. Integration of At-Risk Youth: Israeli Success with
   Youth Aliyah Programs 37
5. Federal Failures: How Bureaucracy Hinders Progress 73
6. Snapshots of Chaos: Personal Portraits of Pittsburgh 83
7. Conclusion 101

Appendix I: Agencies Receiving "Act Together" Grants............................. 105

Appendix II: An Operational Definition of Public Service 111

Appendix III: Behavioral Checklist for Social Integration Attitudes........ 113

Appendix IV: Public Service Commitment Questionnaire B...................... 115

Glossary of Hebrew Terms... 137

Bibliography 141

Index 143

List of Tables

A.1 Spearman Brown Split Half Test Results... 119
A.2 Results of Israeli Army Intelligence Tests for Ramat Hakovesh
 Graduates... 121
A.3 Results on Social Integration Based on Responses to
 Questionnaire A (June-July, 1977) 123
A.4 Results on Upward Social Mobility Based on Leisure Time
 Responses... 125
A.5 Results of the Three Groups' Responses
 Relating to Background, Public Service Commitment,
 Ideology, and Social Adjustment.. 127
A.6 Results on Behavioral Characteristic Categories................................ 131

Preface

I am indebted to many people who assisted me in the creation and writing of <u>Children in Chaos</u>. Joseph Ritter, director of the Social Work Department of the Tel Aviv Municipality, and Aaron Sharon, the social worker who served as liaison to the staff of the Rehabilitation Program (<u>Hachshara Hatzira</u> in Hebrew—see Glossary) at Kibbutz Ramat Hakovesh , both helped me understand the goals of Youth Aliyah programs (see Glossary) in the 1970s.

Yitzchak, Hadas, and Genia, staff members at Ramat Hakovesh, were my most honest and accurate witnesses to the program's ability to integrate at-risk youth in Israel.

I received a great deal of advice and guidance from Dr. Joseph W. Eaton, Dr. Seth Spaulding, and Dr. Alex Weillenmann, all of the University of Pittsburgh.

From 1982–1985, my dedicated colleagues at Three Rivers Youth, Marsha Lewis and Thomas Canada, taught me to understand the concept of high-risk youth and how to work directly with them. Mrs. Ruth Richardson, the executive director of Three Rivers Youth, and Dr. David Droppa, the assistant director, were also my mentors in the 1980s. They gave me their instructive insights and had confidence in my work and professional growth during my attempts to rehabilitate at-risk youth in Pittsburgh.

Robin Rogers, director of research of the Allegheny County Commission for Work Force Excellence, advised me on the difficulties many high-risk youth face in attempting to enter good alternative educational programs.

Many other friends and family members have encouraged and given me their support.

Rabbi Jason Edelstein, a colleague, friend, and adviser, guided me in solving many problems in my day-to-day work with youth. Rabbi Charles Shalman gave enormous time and energy in editing and organizing the book's final form. Carolyn Abla typed and retyped the manuscript until everything was in good order.

My wife Malke was always there to give me her creative advice and make constructive corrections, and also inspired my enthusiasm throughout the year that it took to complete the project. My brother, Ben Frank, inspired me to do what I dreamed to do by saying, "Just sit down and write it." To all of them, I owe a world of gratitude.

Introduction

At a Jewish Educators' Conference in 1991, I sat and listened in amazement to a report about a prestigious Conservative Hebrew camp. On that day, a special recommendation was being made to discreetly attach social workers to the units of all the summer camps, since in recent years family and other socioemotional issues relating directly to the campers' lives had arisen. The situations were so serious that Jewish counselors and directors could not handle them. A few weeks later, I read an article by a director of a Reform Jewish youth camp who wrote, "When I started my career in camping (1974), the words "youth" and "suicide" were rarely used in the same breath. Now we instruct every youth worker in the detection of the all too-common-signs and symptoms of children at risk" (Dobin 1991, 37).

In 1976, I had already discovered a group of street youth at-risk in South Tel Aviv. They would not enter a lavish looking community center for recreation, choosing instead to hang out in the streets nearby, sometimes causing damage to the public property on the street or to the center itself. The city of Tel Aviv had to assign a social worker to them as well; the community center's director, Yitzchak, told me that I should make every effort to attach myself to them and convince them to participate in the community center's activities. Soon after, I did learn that Youth Aliyah, a national agency, had successfully absorbed immigrant youth into Israeli society from Nazi-held territory in the late 1930s, from North Africa in the 1950s, and from the metropolitan poverty-stricken slum areas within Israel in the 1970s. In fact, a Tel Aviv social worker referred me directly to a group of street youth integrated into Israeli society through a unique alternative educational program which had lasted two years in a kibbutz (see Glossary) north of Tel Aviv. This group and other Youth Aliyah groups had participated in Hachshara Hatzira (see Glossary) and had become a unit in a special agricultural paramilitary army training program called Nachal (see Glossary). I did research on this group for four years, using an in-depth case study design for nineteen boys and girls, most of whom had entered and finished the program and were almost ready for their army release in early 1978.

Later in 1982–1983, I began to work with American street youth in Pittsburgh, Pennsylvania, learning to do so in extremely difficult situations. In all cases, the groups' ages were sixteen to twenty. These young people who had some chance to break the poverty-failure-juvenile/adult justice cycle were learning in a unique work and study alternative program, but it was shorter in length than Youth Aliyah programs and lacked the ingredient of a therapeutic follow-up. In late 1983, I wrote a manuscript for the Kibbutz Studies Project at Harvard University, in which I compared some American and Israeli educational programs, all of which had the goal to integrate high-risk youth as constructive citizens into society. As I continued to work with the youth of Pittsburgh in the mid- and late 1980s, I began to realize the depth of the problems of such children. I realized that drugs, being jailed or warehoused in juvenile centers, and early pregnancies or health problems would soon do them in. They would never live positive civilian lives.

The school system had hardly made a dent, nor was it meant to do so. As Jonathan Kozol wrote in The Night is Dark and I Am Far From Home, "United States education is by no means an inept disordered construction. It is an ice-cold and superb machine. Its job is to socialize the good children, not to teach the children of broken homes neither the positive values nor the means by which to survive" (Kozol 1975, 1).

After a long search for positive answers to their problems, I reached the conclusion that without the Youth Aliyah's <u>Hachshara Hatzira</u> program, the nineteen clients of my case study would not have become such ideologically motivated soldiers and eventually good citizens (after their release from the Israeli Army). Only through such programs as the <u>Hachshara Hatzira</u> of Youth Aliyah; Orr Shalom, a special supportive program in Jerusalem; an alternative educational work program in Highfields, New Jersey; and the Three Rivers Youth application of some Youth Aliyah concepts, could caring principals, teachers, counselors, social workers, and therapists change the children who fit the high-risk description.

Since 1976, I have reviewed the case studies of four different groups of such children and worked with some of them in Israel and the United States as well. In a majority of these cases, the youth were not at all successfully integrated into society, nor were many of the individuals whom I met and interviewed who were not in any program. Therefore, it is incumbent on me to define what is meant by the term "high-risk youth." The definition fits millions of the children of America and Israel, children of all races and religions. It is also important to define other terms, such as "integration" and "short-term outdoor programs" before outlining the types of programs, places, environments, and professionals that could help us solve many of the problems. Unless we implement these programs, the chaos of the young lives in this country, in Israel, and in many other countries will overwhelm modern society; we will have more crime and chaos in a world already filled with the pain of such elements.

The term "high-risk youth" can be viewed as an all-encompassing concept which has been used in the 1980s by only a few social agencies and governmental organizations in America as Act Together (a Washington-based organization). Since there are so many negative statements or reactions by young people (aged sixteen to twenty) to society, it is best to analyze the overall concept, first by naming and describing the list of categories into which they fit, and secondly by giving specific examples of the young people whose background and present situations place them in the categories herein presented. This will be done as the story of the American and Israeli youth studied over the last fifteen years unfolds.

The first major category is the "failure syndrome." High-risk youth are rarely able to succeed in school, on the job, in their family relationships, or in the social setting we call society. They often express hopelessness and frustration. They appear sad and angry to the adults they learn to trust. When they are helped, they often become immobilized as the time to use their skills arrive. They are the hardest people to reach and serve! Even after they have acquired skills and have begun to work, they tend to lose jobs, fail again in schools, and become involved in crimes. Many students of short-term training programs had been placed in job positions, but lost them within a space of time not exceeding the training. Thus, the statistics show that many high-risk youth remain in the failure cycle which our society has not yet broken to any significant extent.

In a recent report on the decrease of violent crimes in the United States, it was explained that over half of the crimes were committed by youngsters aged fifteen to twenty-four. The assumption was that only when the "baby boom" generation reaches middle age, and community cooperation, police enforcement, and heavier court deterrents come into play will there be a chance to reduce crime everywhere in the country. Until that time, high-risk youth will use their energy in a nonproductive way. For example, youth under eighteen were arrested for 87,222 violent offenses in 1980, and in 1981 there were 479,000 youths being held in 8,833 adult jails and lockups.

Youngsters who feel inferior, deprived, and frustrated express those feelings through vandalism and stealing. Youth from dysfunctional families often have low academic skills, vague or totally missing career goals, a poor or complete lack of work history, drug and/or alcohol abuse, and involvement with the juvenile justice system. The patterns are clear. Richard E. Desmond of the University of Pittsburgh expressed it well when he wrote: "The community orientation of rehabilitation is appropriate for delinquent youth since many of them have difficulty functioning in the community either because they are acting out their dislikes in the community or because they lack skills needed to function successfully in the community" (Desmond and Smith 1984, 120).

The most common characteristics of the families involved in a survey of high-risk youth are social failure, dependency, disturbed intrafamily relations, and violent methods of child rearing. In human and financial terms, these families account for a large part of the expenditures for public assistance, police involvement, child placement facilities, correctional institutions, and psychological treatment. In general, the trend in America has been to institutionalize homeless or socially maladjusted children. As John Matshushima expressed it, "When hopelessness led to warehousing, the attitudes of the parents and the community perpetuated the role into which the patients were cast" (Matshushima 1977, 47). In the decade between 1960 and 1970, the number of children institutionalized jumped from 282,292 to 298,578. There was also a 45 percent increase in the number of children in mental hospitals and residential treatment centers. These trends were alive in the 1980s and were associated with poverty and unemployment, creating more dysfunctional families on the American scene, creating havoc especially among the black community (Pittsburgh Press, December 7, 1983, 1). The unemployment-poverty conditions have impacted heavily on families with young people already facing the failure syndrome. It is therefore obvious that such descriptive adjectives as "antisocial," "hostile," "mistrustful," "cynical," and "apathetic" have their roots in the institutions of our society, and it will take many caring individuals a long period of time to root them out. With the overall cooperation of the society in which they have been nurtured, plus more motivating activities over a long period of time to create an educational process of benefit, the invisible youth could climb out of the abyss of depressing poverty and despair.

To confirm the definition of high-risk youth and the statistics given the reader in the above paragraphs, I quote a 1991 Congressional Report (Office of Technology Assessment): "One-fourth of our kids are at very high risk and half are at higher than normal risk," said David Hamburg, president of Carnegie Corporation of New York, which assisted the Congressional O.T.A. Among other things, the report also shows that youngsters most in need of help have little access to the services that could make a difference in their lives. Perhaps even more damaging "to the youngsters and to society as a whole" was the large number of adolescents who engage in self-destructive behavior that limits their futures, such as sexual promiscuity, alcohol and substance abuse, careless driving, dropping out of school and delinquency (Aiken, April 23, 1991, 1). Another report in the same newspaper stated that one out of four high school youths thought about suicide, and one out of twelve actually tried it (Killackey, September 20, 1991, 1).

At this point, such a report should not be a surprise but a confirmation of the chaos and our inability to halt it with the available services.

1
Changing Youths' Attitudes: Well-meaning Attempts in the United States

I'm the boy with the smileless laugh
and the girl much too old for her time

Audra L. Bagley

On March 6, 1984, B. W., a twenty-year-old on probation, turned up at the Three Rivers Youth Center in Pittsburgh, Pennsylvania, and offered to wash and polish my car. He did not finish it that first Friday, so he offered to return the next week. He eventually washed my car twice, the second time creating not a small amount of anxiety on my part, since he and the 1976 Ford disappeared for a few hours. (He later told me that he had gone to find some rags needed to complete the job, but it took him a little longer than he thought it would.) He also went far in the program, since he developed enough trust in us to stay until September and earn an "unofficial" completion certificate. He will be mentioned again in Chapter 6.

Y. A. of Tel Aviv, Israel, lived in a poor neighborhood in South Tel Aviv, across from the Barbour Community Center. His father was a policeman, his mother a housewife. They were born in Iraq. He finished the ninth grade and then left high school and had part-time jobs until 1976. When I met him in the winter of 1976, he was a well-known leader of the Barbour street group and considered himself "a sometimes member" of the center as far back as 1971. He had not paid membership since 1975. He was twice arrested for breaking and entering apartments in Tel Aviv. He had a parole officer who visited him and occasionally spoke to the social coordinator of Barbour about Y's behavior. He never joined or related in any significant way to an alternative educational program. He remained an at-risk youth for the three years after he entered the Israeli Army in 1977.

Neither of these youngsters had been integrated into their society, yet both had been physically and even spiritually located on the fringes of an alternative program which could have helped them to be absorbed as decent citizens into society.

In Israel, the problem of integrating such young people goes back three decades. During that time, a system of ethnic stratification had crystallized in Israel, a system of structured inequality in the things that count in the society, closely pinned to ethnicity. No matter what researchers use as an indicator of socioeconomic class, they find a consistent and high correlation between class and ethnicity. The Eastern Jews of Israel, also known as Sepharadim (see Glossary), are heavily concentrated in the lower social strata, regardless of length of stay in Israel. Even the young Sabras (native-born Israelis) among them differ from the Western Jews, also known as Ashkenazim (see Glossary), in their perception of opportunities for advancement.

This last supposition formed the focus of my original study, since the gap in the late 1970s between Sabras whose parents were born in the East and those of European-born parents had become greater than the gap between young immigrants from the two geographic areas. Despite a slightly growing rate of intermarriage documented in the 1950s and 1960s, Israelis born of European parents deviate from the pattern of increased intermarriage and their inclination to marry within the group has been strengthened. Finally, the real fear of most researchers and the Eastern leadership is that ethnic stratification will grow as the more successful members of the Eastern stratum intermarry. The dominant group will be mixed as the subordinate group will be predominately Eastern.

When I attempted to analyze the concept of integration in the relation to such young people as B. W. and Y. A. and how that could have been accomplished in long-term educational programs in Israel or in the United States, I knew that a theory of integration and social change had to be included as a foundation from which to understand goals of successful educational alternative programs. As many sociologists in the United States and Israel already knew, the rate of illiteracy among teenagers was extremely high (for example, 200 of every 70,000 in every high school grade in Israel). However, children were promoted every year because of teacher/principal sympathy, or because it was hoped that the child would do better next year.

There was high functional illiteracy even in the Israeli Army among Eastern Jewish youth. The Commander-in-Chief, Rafael Eitan, spoke of 30,000 to 40,000 illiterates (the Israeli Army entrance age was eighteen) who had received only four years of schooling. Israeli Army officials claimed that poor environmental conditions had allowed the type of illiteracy to be passed on from one generation to another and this was another example of the social gap which still existed in Israel. By 1985, statistics showed that the median number of school years for Eastern Israeli male youth was six compared to nine for Western Israelis and four to nine for the females of the two ethnic blocs. In the United States, literacy programs proliferated in the 1970-1990 period, due to the fact that caring educators began to understand the extent of the illiteracy problem.

In connecting such educational and social statistics in the late 1970s and into the decade of the 1980s to the integration and social change theory, I began to discover that scholars such as Roy Prodipto and Fred Heyward contributed to the measurement of integration by developing an "Index of Integration" by which "political activities" of participants could be scored. Their theory, which allowed certain social or political activity to receive integration points, was reinforced by political journalist Sarah Honig. In 1975, she wrote in the Jerusalem Post Magazine that studies in Israel demonstrated that ethnic group's integration could be related directly to the group's political activities, such as demonstrations, meetings of organizations, and even formal membership in an organization which was politically active (Honig 1975, 5).

After World War II, social scientists such as Shmuel Eisenstadt and Walter Rostow had applied neoevolutionary models to Third World countries and had described states that people had to pass before educational change could be implemented on an incremental basis. Later, however, a new type of paradigm made up of new theories and representing new social forces gained ascendancy. The new power groups believed that dramatic social change is a basic element of educational change. They believed such nonformal educational methods are related directly to economic, political, and social change in the developing countries, and in the marginal rural and urban populations of the United States, Israel, and other Western countries. They would focus on social change phenomena and theories both in the social and educational spheres.

The establishment would have to tolerate such changes in order to bring about the integration of "disadvantaged" people. In general, the conflict theorists had seen social change occurring due to the rise of groups which responded to the need for more scarce resources; this held true for Marxist and non-Marxist. Some social change theoreticians, such as Applebaum, believed that societies had to crack the societal frame which oppressed them and their traditional educational systems before the real chains of colonialism could be broken. Cultural revitalization movements as among Black Muslims and Native Americans have sought access to scarce resources, and they have used educational methods to achieve their goals.

Ivan Ilich seeks to free individuals from the established institutions which develop expectations among the poor that society does not fulfill. In education, Ilich would open up creative alternatives to develop spiritually free people who would control societal resources. These theories in general have helped to shape recent educational approaches that are oriented toward social change, and in many ways they apply to the peer group approach of the Youth Aliyah Rehabilitation Program.

In the last three decades, there have been a number of examples of so-called encampments for youth which were initiated to influence attitudes toward social integration. In the early 1960s, Charles Hyman and Louis Wright finished their research evaluation on a six-week encampment program of

1955. In their sociological study <u>Encampment for Citizenship</u>, they reached the conclusion that attempts to change attitudes of young Americans so as to enhance socially integrative behavior are only successful for a short period (six weeks or so) after the youngsters reach home. However, four years later the drop in percentage was great enough to return the attitude scale scores to the pre-camp level as of six weeks before the program began (Hyman and Wright 1962, 271–272).

Since the environmental effects of socioeconomic class of the participants, the interests of teachers and administrators, parental attitudes, and neighborhood mores all play a relevant role in the final long-range outcomes of such programs, Hyman and Wright emphasized the need for extended programs so that during longer periods of time, new and unique educational methods and communication between the participants and other population sectors could be utilized in achieving the "higher purpose" of social integration.

An evaluation by Robert Millward of Pennsylvania State University, entitled <u>Outdoor Education</u> (1970), analyses the outcome of encampment activities in racially integrated outdoor settings in western Pennsylvania. In his evaluation, the author suggested that involvement in specific programs in integrative settings enhanced socially integrative behavior, but that later environmental factors such as parental and peer group attitudes, neighborhood settings, and teacher and administrative insensitivity would advance behavioral patterns not indicative of social integration.

Due to these qualifications, the threshold concept of Phillip E. Jacob and Henry Teune (authors of <u>The Integration of Political Communities</u>) whereby an arbitrary point of integration could be fixed by the amount of activities, was relevant to any study of outdoor encampment-type programs which existed over an extended period of time in a highly ideologically supportive environment. Jacob and Teune also asked certain specific questions which could measure the cohesiveness of a society and the concept of integration generally: "How many things must people do together to be integrated? How persistently must they do these common tasks?" (Jacob and Teune 1964, preface).

In the well-known book <u>The Nerves of Government</u>, Karl Deutsch analyzed the processes which organizations pass through in their attempts to reach higher purposes. Organizations, such as the Youth Aliyah Agency, while receiving positive feedback to continue more or less on the same path toward a higher goal, would create various changes at normative, strategic, and operational levels as they moved from one to another intermediate goal to reach a higher goal. As a few other educational agencies in the United States and in other areas of the world, Youth Aliyah constantly was influenced by the environmental factors to which they adapted; while they were adapting and creating changes, they strove to reach the higher purpose of social integration for the at-risk youth in their care.

By 1978, it was apparent to me that the outdoor programs in California, western Pennsylvania, and Michigan were not isolated from the surrounding environments. They were sensitive to the immediate needs of certain segments of the population, and streams of information coming into them induced their leadership to shift previous intermediate goals and develop plans and new goals toward which to strive. However, unlike Youth Aliyah programs during the 1950–1970 period of crises in Israel's youth culture, the outdoor alternatives in America did not establish extended programs which could change social or behavioral attitudes.

In Israel, by the 1960s, the goal had become "pluralistic integration," a most realistic process to reach the goal of social integration. Then the social and educational goals became: personal contact which would lead to the reduction of prejudices between ethnic clusters; a more positive attitude toward others on the part of the disadvantaged population as they became more personally adjusted in society; and the increasing achievements (closing the gap) of the disadvantaged minority groups. This was the focus of Youth Aliyah. In addition, it was in tune with the environment and understood the amount of time necessary to reach its educational and social goals. As it has been documented in Israel and now in the United States, it was to be one of very few alternative educational programs to integrate high-risk youth into the patterns of good behavior and positive attitudes toward the society.

2
Warehousing Our Children:
Another Dismal Failure

It's me, the child of the universe,
though I hang out and lie in the street.

Audra L. Bagley

B. S. called me collect from Pittsburgh, ten blocks away from
the Oakland Center of Three Rivers Youth's Alternative
Educational Vocational Program (A.E.V.P.). He was one of
the first students in the North Side A.E.V.P. He always had
creative energy. He loved to draw, but after he graduated from
our GED (Graduate Equivalent Degree) program, he began to
fail miserably in a business school. One day, he had told
Marsha, our very capable therapist, and me that he was desperate for money, since he needed to buy milk for his girlfriend's
baby. He was going to sell his books and go back on welfare,
but he lacked the patience to get a financial officer of the
school to sign the papers. He was also on our list to help find a
part-time job. Before attempting to help him stay in school, we
gave him bus fare to get home and back to school the next
week, and Marsha gave him an extra few dollars to buy milk
and groceries. On that day, August 12, 1983, we knew that we
had talked him out of stealing.

He did go for a few job interviews later in the month, but was
not hired by a Pittsburgh company at that time. Finally, he did
get a part-time job, and I was able to speak to Mr. D., the
president of the business school, who allowed him to make up
work in September. In that month, our program ended, but
unofficially I continued to help B. S., W. G., T. W., D. H., and
R. C. to solve their problems, some of which were with law

enforcement agencies. Many of the students did enter junior colleges or business schools, and most of them enjoyed learning about the world they had never experienced. When B. S. called me in July 1984, he had just returned from New York City. He had worked in New York as a dishwasher, he claimed, but desperation was on his doorstep again. He had studied one semester at Duff's, failed his studies by January, and dropped out.

Marsha felt that he was the one boy my family should take in, but also knew it was impractical. This time I was tempted to talk to my wife about the idea, but on advice from Marsha and others, I suggested to B. S. that he go out on his own and find a job in the area until he could get himself together. By October 1984, the majority of our students were somehow surviving, but many were still in the ranks of the poor, probably to be stuck there until they died. We lacked the funds for professional follow-up, and the societal support had not been forthcoming. B. S. did get a job in the Oakland area of Pittsburgh, and I did see him twice working in a major supermarket that year. However, by 1985 he was calling me to lend him ten dollars, and soon after that, he again called me, this time from a hospital where he had admitted himself for drug addiction. He would end up institutionalized, just like 300,000 other young people who had been homeless and socially maladjusted in the preceding decades.

At least 105,000 youths in the 1970s had reached correctional institutions, a figure which had risen 17,000 from the previous decade. There had also been a 45 percent increase in numbers of children in mental institutions or residential treatment centers. As the statistics told the story of more, rather than less, institutionalization for children, the sociological results of such treatment clearly confirmed that other systems of care for homeless and socially maladjusted children were needed. The "Interaction Model" at Highfields, one of the potentially successful residential rehabilitation programs in the United States, was a manifestation of American social workers' and educators' awareness of the need for better answers.

In the late 1960s, it was reported that 2,138 public and private residential institutions in the United States, Puerto Rico, and the Virgin Islands existed for children and that 701 facilities for mentally retarded and 373 for the physically handicapped brought the grand total to 3,212 institutions for children in the United States and its territories. No one institution was, or is now able to treat the variety of children who require care and are either homeless or so alienated from their families and society that they cannot live within those realms of modern life. For this reason, by 1970, social workers and educators began to look for other answers.

In the Youth Aliyah scheme of things, the term "rehabilitation" was used to denote a plan which was carried out under the supervision of a social worker and an educational supervisor. The Youth Rehabilitation Program is one of many programs carried out for clients who are rated (after many interviews with them, and with family, friends, and teachers, and after examining medical and psychological reports) as eligible to receive services for rehabilitation. It has been established to provide semi-skilled job opportunities in a highly democratic society based on the moral values of equality, respect for labor, decency, devotion to crucial national issues, and a natural tendency to contribute to the environment.

Early in the absorption process into the program, social workers have discussions with the youth in order to encourage positive motivations and reinforce the self-image of the individual and the group to improve its cohesiveness around a common goal. As the program begins to develop in the kibbutz, individual treatment to provide a variety of satisfactions which meet the human basic needs and promote social adjustment is emphasized. Joseph Ritter has elaborated on this rehabilitation approach by adding that there are at least four other levels which assist in the rehabilitation of Youth Aliyah's socially maladjusted clients.

The levels of work, education, group socialization, and community or environment are necessary ingredients in rehabilitating socially maladjusted youngsters in Youth Aliyah programs, and it is on these levels that other programs outside of Israel have begun to focus as well (Ritter 1973, 3).

There were nineteen youths who would have been institutionalized in one way or another if they had not attended the Youth Aliyah Rehabilitation Program in Ramat Hakovesh. In these cases there are distinct similarities to young people like B. S., not only because the Israeli children were born into ethnic minority groups as he was, but also because the high-risk criteria fit them perfectly. As I interviewed them and researched their backgrounds, it was apparent to me that 100 percent had been born into dysfunctional Eastern families. The following brief descriptions will give the reader a clear view of the characteristics which placed the young people at risk at age sixteen or less.

Y. D. was in a family of eleven children, which was under great tension due to the mother's lack of patience. Y. D. had been at a boarding school for two years and had been described as very quiet and depressed there, since no one from his family visited him. At Ramat Hakovesh, he was described as creative and an average achiever although still relatively shy during the first year. In the Israeli Army, he scored fifty-one, which is a point above average, even though he had only finished eighth grade in public school. He was never A.W.O.L. and he was considered a responsible front line soldier.

Y. S. was a member of a family of eight children. In October 1975, the Tel Aviv social workers were already watching his progress in school. At that time he was in eighth grade. He apparently was in trouble with many teachers. In January 1975, he was sent to Youth Aliyah's Kelet course (see Glossary) to prepare him for the Ramat Hakovesh program, and he joined it officially in June 1975 at age sixteen. He was involved and very popular in the program. In June 1976, he was an active partici- pant in a show put on by the whole group for the Kibbutz. In April 1977, he was rated an "outstanding student" in a gadna practice (see Glossary). In the army, he became a sergeant, commanding a small unit. He was never A.W.O.L. and scored a sixty-one on the Army Intelligence Test.

L. A. was a young lady in a family of six children living in the Tikvah quarter. She had quit school before entering ninth grade. Her mother was constantly sick and her father sent her to the Social Work Department in Tel Aviv since she was not studying or working. She passed the one-year preparation course (Kelet) as an outstanding student, did well at Ramat Hakovesh, and then joined the Nachal with twelve other gradu- ates of the Youth Aliyah Program at Ramat Hakovesh. In the army, she was never A.W.O.L. and was given a clerical position after scoring sixty-two on the intelligence test.

As I continued to review the Israeli Army records of the origi- nal Ramat Hakovesh Group, I marvelled at the results, the outcome of a program with one counselor, one teacher, and one housemother. However, when I added the ingredients of time and space (i.e., two years of thousands of caring hours and a highly ideological supportive environment filled with voting kibbutz members who had chosen in their general meeting to take on the project), I understood what happened during that period in the Israeli <u>Nachal</u> unit. Y. S., Y. D. and L. A. had a double advantage over B. S.: two years in the Ramat Hakovesh program, plus more integrative education from the Israeli Army. This was facilitated because Israeli society believes in social integration. It still remained for me, however, to use scholarly research methods in order to discover the actual behavioral and attitudinal changes for the Israeli youth, as well as whether there were programs in the United States which had the same potential to create change.

3
Some Good Educational Programs: A Brief Overview

On April 19, 1991, President George Bush made a speech in the East Room of the White House, encouraging local communities to build high quality American schools. What did he say about local communities' strategies that could bring the large numbers of at-risk teenagers off the streets into work and study programs for a year or more? He did not put forward new ideas. In the 1980s–1990s, the level of awareness to educate the whole child over an extended period of time has not been high among government policymakers in the United States. Their narrowing down of programs to a minimum number of performance contracts with a few dedicated social agencies has diminished the ability of our professional social workers and educators to use all their tools to accomplish the tasks which were vital.

I was told in 1989 that the executive director of J.T.P.A. (Job Training Partnership Act) in an industrial Eastern city claimed that there were not enough disadvantaged youth in the ghettos of this well-known urban renaissance metropolis to warrant the development of job and study alternative educational programs. Of course, he was referring to his estimate that there was a shortage of high-risk adolescent youth to recruit for programs.

In this chapter, contrary to such administrator's rationalizations, there will be an enumeration of the dire needs of America's youth and of some unique educational approaches in our country to locate and to help the invisible children in those chaotic streets during the last two decades. Such programs have provided a limited amount of assistance for hundreds of children. A few of them used residential educational models as well as the training of committed staff members and the application of caring attitudes to well-developed educational methods.

In the 1980s, Act Together (a non-profit organization based in Washington, DC) was able to give some large grants to a dozen worthy social agencies which had proposed excellent programs for high-risk youth in the United States. Some other agencies in this country and a few in Israel actually took children off the streets and from their dysfunctional families and placed them in long-term peer group educational work programs. In this way, it was realized that such young people have an opportunity to become responsible citizens in our society.

In Pittsburgh, the Three Rivers Youth program tried to do in six months in its A.E.V.P. (Alternative Educational Vocational Program) in a nonresidential setting what Youth Aliyah programs accomplished in supportive environments—ideologically-oriented pioneering ones to be exact. For Youth Aliyah graduates of the two-year kibbutz programs, the environment was an essential element in relation to their attitudinal and behavioral changes.

Youth Aliyah residents lived in cooperative peer group situations, studying and working for at least two years in one comprehensive program. Although Three Rivers Youth developed a highly integrated service system, which included a well-organized educational and vocational component, the latter was for a much shorter period of time; its urban environment of Pittsburgh, where the Three Rivers Youth base still exists, caused difficulties which were never completely overcome.

In the 1970s, unique outdoor programs had been established in western Pennsylvania to improve racial intergroup relations. The Western Pennsylvania Programs Emergency School Aid Act (E.S.A.A.) in Pittsburgh and the A.E.V.P. prepared participants for full-time jobs after the completion of the six-month program. Its unique educational program, which was lauded by Act Together as part of an integrated service system of Three Rivers Youth (T.R.Y.), also used an intergroup peer group behavioral modification model and it did receive positive feedback from probation officers and employers who had hired T.R.Y. youth in late 1983 and early 1984.

The "invisible youth" had learned enough in six months to pass G.E.D. (Graduate Equivalent Diploma) tests, acquire interviewing and application skills, as well as some life skills; for example, budgeting, grooming, and others which no one had ever tried to teach them. Many of the youngsters entered post-secondary schools by September 1983 or January 1984 (sixty-five young people were helped between November 1982 and September 1983). In fact, 80 percent of those tested received G.E.D.s and 65 percent worked part time or full time or entered school at Connelley Skill Learning Center, Community College, Duff's Business Institute, or other institutions of learning. By 1986, however, only a few of these students had professional certificates or diplomas. In October 1983, I was able to follow up on the placement statistics. I felt the need to do some investigative research as a support person and also to learn for myself where the young people would be in their lives by 1986.

My immediate assumption in the summer of 1984, was that statistics mean very little and that the pattern of life of such high-risk youth cannot be reduced to a purely statistical social science. We tend to worship our educational and social sciences. At that time, I also felt that grants should not be readily given out to even idealistic programs which were less than a year old, no matter how concerned the agency was that developed them. This was true in the 1950s and certainly it remained true in the late 1970s. However, by the 1980s, it had become apparent that funds for follow-up programming could help these agencies deliver the services which high-risk youth desperately needed.

Many of the short encampment peer group programs in America, such as the E.S.A.A. program, did rely purely on group interaction through a variety of educational methods which were aimed at attitudinal changes. However, most of them were not extended and could not meet the criterion of influencing the participants at all of the levels which were so beneficial to young people. Youth Aliyah's Rehabilitation Program in Kibbutz was able to reach all the necessary levels. The evaluation of the staff of E.S.A.A. well summarized their shortcoming: "We all felt that we had to coordinate camp programs with the school activities much more. We could not reach the ultimate goals we had set" (Frank, July 1975, 1).

The "Interaction Model" of the Highfields Peer Group Work Project, as well as a number of alternative educational rehabilitation programs recommended by Act Together, worked well with juvenile delinquents outside the institutional setting, and were successful in rehabilitating high-risk youth if they were extended beyond a year. They also succeeded when their goal orientation was similar to Youth Aliyah's programs in Israeli kibbutzim. The "Interaction Model" postulated that:

(1) the delinquent will change his behavior in presocial direction only if such conduct is acceptable to his peer group;
(2) the change is most effectively achieved if the entire peer group is the target of change;
(3) change will occur through a process of integration with others who are also changing in the program.

This peer group behavior modification concept served as a possible feature toward social rehabilitation.

These programs by necessity included committed staffs and supportive societal efforts of the communities where they existed—just as Youth Aliyah's efforts of the 1970s included similar elements. Without all of these special features, the best educational and vocational peer group programs could not get the job done in the 1970s, nor in the 1980s.

The story of one partially successful work and study program can now be honestly narrated. Many of the heroes and heroines of that Three Rivers Youth A.E.V.P. had been residents of group homes and the slums of Pittsburgh. Many of them had juvenile records, low reading levels (first to sixth grade), had difficulty filling out the simple job applications, often looked depressed, and were usually inappropriately dressed. This was not unusual for the young people of the 1980s, although in 1982 the silence about the subject was very real. There were sixty-five students such as B. S. and B. W. in that 1982–1983 Program. (B. S. and B. W. are mentioned in Chapters 2 and 6.)

All of the young people lived in environments which consisted of families who were not only poor but were also unable to motivate their children to better themselves. Therefore, their own capabilities and the environmental potential to aid them were very limited. As a result, their reaction to the society with which they could not cope was negative. The young people did not believe they could ever succeed and became frightened when they approached one chance to be placed in a job or registered at a career school or college. This concept was referred to as the "Fear of Success Syndrome."

It had taken our staff a good deal of time just to break down the students' defenses as they initially distrusted all adults–even ones who were working to help them. They did eventually become close to some staff members as they learned to trust them. They became gradually "hooked" into the program because of our efforts. At least, this was what we would have liked to believe. There were many students who returned to visit us often in 1984 in order to seek support and help, and they allowed us to attempt to convince them to become part of a therapeutic program. Many of these students called us from jail or from outside the city while in crisis situations: i.e., losing their dwelling places, lacking nourishment for their babies, or being ill. Often they were desperate enough to steal.

By the end of the first cycle, a high percentage of those young people who did hold full-time or part-time jobs while attending a post-secondary school began to appear on paper as positive statistics. In July 1983, another cycle placed 95 percent of its students.

The staff of these programs continually tried to orient the clients to work by placing them on jobs with nonprofit organizations soon after the orientation periods ended. Every student worked three or four days a week and had at least one interview for a part-time or full-time job. However, some of these participants never did leave their street lives (one who was working at a police station tried to keep it a secret from his friends on the corner); nor did they escape from the cycle of poverty. Since they were depressed, they doubted if they could ever succeed. By the end of the first A.E.V.P. (October 1983), only a small percentage did find a way to use the chance to succeed in the long run. Some of them were still trying to do just that in 1988.

However, unless community leaders can provide the funds for trained social workers and educators to establish extended residential programs, including both work and study programs in very supportive environments, the vast majority of these young people will remain invisible until their poverty and despair lead to crime and violence.

Knowledge and sensitivity about what needs to be done must not only be keen, it must also be activated. Lip service, which is a method of keeping one's distance or landing a few positive statistics, will not accomplish the goal in the long run.

The Youth Aliyah Rehabilitation Program, carried out for clients who are rated as eligible to receive services for rehabilitation, was established to provide semi-skilled job opportunities in a highly democratic society based on moral values of equality, respect for labor, decency, devotion to crucial national issues, and a natural tendency to contribute to the environment. Early in the absorption process into this unique educational program, social workers have discussions with the youth in order to encourage positive motivations and to reinforce the self-image of the individual and the group to improve its cohesiveness around a common goal. As the peer group program began to develop in the kibbutz, individual treatment to provide a variety of satisfactions which meet basic human needs and promote social adjustment was provided. Mr. Ritter, the director of the Social Work Department in Tel Aviv, emphasized at least four other areas which aid in the rehabilitation process. The areas of work, education, group socialization, and community or environment are necessary ingredients in rehabilitating the clients; and outside of Israel, programs that work on these levels have also begun to succeed.

The results of the peer group program at Highfields, as well as those of a few other unique educational rehabilitation programs, a number of which were commended by Act Together for being highly successful in rehabilitating high risk youth (see Appendix I) prove that there is a potential contribution of other residential educational programs similar in goal orientation, education processes, commitment of staff, and supportive societal efforts to that which Youth Aliyah established in Israeli kibbutzim in the 1970s. Finally, the peer group program at Highfields made attempts at the group socialization level to help socially maladjusted youth achieve the goal of social rehabilitation.

As in the Youth Aliyah's Kibbutz Rehabilitation Program, the Highfields, New Jersey's "Interaction Model" combined a strong peer group working program in a supportive community. It had enough funding and community backing to allow youth who had been involved with the juvenile justice system to change their attitudes and behavioral patterns to a great enough extent to be socially rehabilitated.

In Israel, a unique Army program involving special training for ill-educated delinquents and near-delinquents, continues, although lately funding has become a serious problem. "Truth be told, the Israeli Defense Forces does not need teenage trouble-makers, but they need the I.D.F. (Israeli Defense Forces)" (Myers, July 28, 1991, 15). It is almost impossible for a young man to acquire a decent job in the country without evidence that he has done military service and been granted an honorable discharge. Two groups, one functionally illiterate and the other with a grade school education, either learn military skills and basic educational subjects for five months or just concentrate for three months on military skills in order to complete the three-year service to their country.

They all come from slum neighborhoods, where their peers believe that only soldiers serve in the Israeli Army. "Their families are hardly functional," one counselor said. Naomi, a counselor, recalled that, "There was a boy whose father served as a pimp for his mother" (Myers).

Although the Israeli Army could send these recruits to do

such simple tasks as washing dishes or sweeping floors in army offices, the principle of investing substantial sums to teach them a specific skill to be used in civilian life has been adopted. Many of these young men with a very limited education have learned carpentry or metal work; the top few have learned how to operate heavy mechanical equipment because they are now capable of reading instruction manuals. Only one-third drop out, ". . . but two-thirds finish their three years of military service and go on to earn an honest living in civilian life—instead of ending up, in all probability, as drug addicts or criminals" (Myers). The program has been facing serious reductions recently but has received the support of an ex-Chief of Staff and present Agriculture Minister Raphael Eitan, who said, "It is inconceivable that the Army should ignore the social problems of the State. Instead of being dropped, the program should be expanded because it today encompasses only one quarter of those who could benefit from it" (Myers, July 28, 1991, 15).

One graduate agreed. He was Avraham who had a difficult time persuading the Army to accept him in the first place because he had been convicted of assault and battery. "Today," he said, "I'm just not the same person I was a few months ago. Who would have believed then that I would allow someone to shout at me and order me around without busting him in the mouth? I used my fists to gain respect; now I get respect with my uniform" (Myers). In this case, as in many others in such programs, an attitude changed as a special environment with an educational-vocational curriculum was able to create a new opportunity for him. The three-year Israeli service period would complete the rehabilitation of this young man and other young soldiers with serious emotional and educational problems.

In Edmond, a suburb of Oklahoma City, Oklahoma, the Boy's Ranch Town Program has existed since 1953. This special educational program was established for boys nine to fourteen years old. Its goal is to rehabilitate youth, or as the Director stated, "To provide a caring environment where boys learn to care for themselves and have a Christ-like love for others."

Thirty percent of the students in this program were below

the poverty line, and fifty percent had families which were described as part of the working poor. Of the fifty young boys ages nine to fourteen who stay at Boy's Ranch one year on an average, fifty percent have been abused. There are not any ethnic or racial monopolies. Since the ranch was Baptist at its inception, one might assume that all the boys come from Baptist families. This is not true. Neither is it a fact that the courts ordered these children, many of whom have become the abusers, to serve time at the ranch. There is a special relationship with Edmond, where the boys went to public school and church, and a unique bonding at the school, where the coordinators of the four branches were also house fathers and mothers and cooks for each cottage. Each child at first spent an average of one to two weeks in a Transitional Boy's Ranch School Program, which is at the facility.

This is a parallel program to the Youth Aliyah Rehabilitation's Kelet (absorption) programs, which are organized at Israeli Army bases. The other interesting similarity is that the program's ideological content of religious values serve the same purpose as the kibbutz value system, motivating the young people toward volunteerism and peer group sharing of community work and its results. At the Boy's Ranch, rodeo programs resulted from work with horses, cattle, sheep, and pigs. The devotional services and the relations at work, which were discussed at group time, played a major role in inspiring community spirit.

Another major work-study program in a highly supportive environment is Cal Farley's Ranch, located west of Amarillo, Texas, on the Canadian River. There, 406 boys and 180 adult employees form a working alternative to delinquent centers for thirteen years—from ages four to eighteen. Established in 1939, the ranch sits on 5,000 acres of land and produces enough food for all the inhabitants. Two married couples, working in alternating shifts, create family structure; in general, discipline at work on the ranch and in school is very strict. Youth who study hard and pass all the subjects through the high school years receive tuition and expenses for any college to which they are accepted.

In the school, there are courses in building trades; there are vocational, agricultural, auto mechanics and carpentry teachers. Every young person, besides his work in agriculture and with animals, must study one vocational subject for four years in high school. The academic curriculum is a regular one and includes Spanish and Latin. The program also has three career guidance counselors for the majority of students who do not go to college. The school is nondenominational, but a new Protestant chapel was recently there. The courts do not intern children there, rather one parent or guardian must apply for the son's entrance. The boy must be of average IQ and be in good health. This program has had some successes, helping some children reach college and others learn a trade while remaining off the street and in a supportive family and community environment for several years.

Orr Shalom was founded in 1980 to meet the needs of Israeli children living outside their home for social reasons. Without including the Youth Aliyah Rehabilitation Program in Kibbutzim, Hachshara Hatzira, it was estimated that 45,000 children lacked individual attention in Israel in 1987, since they had been placed in child care facilities serving 100 children or more. Orr Shalom organized its first therapeutic group in 1979 for homeless, deprived, abused, and neglected children in Israel. The innovative program was based on the philosophy that homeless children have the right to more than a place to sleep and eat. They need professional help with their emotional problems, and more importantly, a loving and caring family atmosphere to give them an opportunity to grow, develop, and integrate into the mainstream of Israeli life.

Since its founding, Orr Shalom has quadrupled the number of children it serves, operating five homes for fifty children in the Jerusalem area. Although it has grown, its objectives have remained the same—to provide troubled children with a secure, caring home, together with needed professional services (psychological counseling, vocational training, and special educational tutoring). The single-family homes are headed by married couples who serve as houseparents. They are parents themselves who have shown an ability to love and care for children.

Each house is home for eight to ten children. In three of the homes they are mixed in regard to age and sex. Orr Shalom accepts sibling groups to enable family units to stay together. The children learn in local schools and return to their Orr Shalom home at the end of the school day. A professional tutor works in the afternoon with the children who need extra help with their homework.

Orr Shalom also encourages the children to interact with the community in which they live and arranges for their participation in local youth groups and in activities at local community centers. Orr Shalom's children have participated in drama, dance, football, and judo classes, and they enjoy swimming in community pools on a regular basis. Like Boy's Ranch, the supporting environment in which the children live is fused with the community outside of it.

A professionally trained social worker supervises the houseparents, meets individually and in groups with the children of each house, and maintains contact with the children's schools. Also, additional support services of cooking and cleaning personnel are provided, so that the houseparents can focus on the children's emotional and physical needs.

By establishing stable homes within the community, Orr Shalom has had a profound impact on the lives of deprived children, contributing to their growth as healthy and productive citizens. Those who are graduates have grown up to serve in the army, complete vocational training, and marry and set up their own homes—in short, work and live as normal and productive members of society.

Friendship House was established in 1984 at the request of the Ministry of Social Affairs. This special project of Orr Shalom has developed an extensive, specialized staff consisting of houseparents, four professional child care workers, two teachers, a social worker, and a psychologist who work with this special population.

The children of Friendship House, all under thirteen years of age, had been through the gamut of social services; no institution had succeeded in reaching them. The majority of the young children had been living in the streets, without hope for the future. Many of the boys had been remanded by the courts, and it was generally expected that they would be sent to locked institutions. However, at Friendship House, due to the special treatment program and expanded staff, the children live in an open home within the community. Working with these children is very difficult, but the staff has shown that it can reach those children that larger, traditional institutions had long given up on.

Orr Shalom's programs are very expensive to operate, yet have been evaluated as the best investment in the long run. The individualized treatment and family-oriented program is the most effective model to break the cycle of delinquency and institutionalization, according to its supporters. They believe that the majority of the graduates of the program will go on to live normal lives. They will also have the tools to bring up their own children without public assistance.

Bob Fenton explained that the aim of Orr Shalom is to keep the children within the community, rather than to place them in a large institution.

Rabbi Harold Kushner, American author of <u>When Bad Things Happen to Good People</u> and a member of the Orr Shalom Overseas Advisory Board, has called Orr Shalom's fourth home, Friendship House, "Israel at its best—patient, caring and compassionate." Harold and Suzette Kushner, and the International Jewish Vegetarian Society, helped raise the funds to establish Friendship House and the special education school on its premises.

Orr Shalom is an independent organization, not affiliated with any political, religious, or government body. It is licensed by the Israel Ministry of Social Affairs. Its homes maintain a traditional religious approach, where candles are lit and Kiddush is recited on Friday night. Both the Orr Shalom family and the natural family come together to celebrate a Bar Mitzvah at the Western Wall.

Houseparents can point out the children who grew up in the Orr Shalom family and are now doing their army service, when they might have ended up roaming the streets. They can show pictures of a young woman, married and with a baby of her own, who learned how to provide a stable, loving home at Orr Shalom.

One can see the names of the young men and women who graduated from vocational schools with an occupational skill to help them get established in life, and hear about the kids who keep coming back to visit, to let their Orr Shalom family know how they're getting along.

The success of Orr Shalom is manifested too in the recognition it received from the Jerusalem Municipality, which suggested that Orr Shalom open an additional family-oriented project, "to apply its characteristic flexibility and innovative techniques to other groups of children" (Jerusalem Post, March 18, 1991, 6). Another article detailed the program and included a study of how in 1986 a girl from Orr Shalom visited her housefather's parents at Byer Home for the Aged, and they became her surrogate grandparents. They eventually died, but the connection made at that point expanded into a volunteer project of Orr Shalom (Ungar, July 24, 1987, 13).

In the summer of 1987, four more girls volunteered to give up two weeks of their vacation to work there. They assisted senior citizens to walk and eat, coaxed smiles out of them, and laughed with them. M., aged fifteen, said that she put perfume on them and combed their hair (Ungar, July 24, 1987, 13).

In summary, this unique family-oriented program inside of the City of the Prophets, Jerusalem, became so successful that such a scholar as Dr. Anita Weiner of Haifa University was commissioned by the Joint Distribution Committee to study its methods and results. In her survey of Orr Shalom's graduates, beginning with the first group of 1980, she found that they had been leading successful lives. "The data collected demonstrated a significant improvement among the graduates in their social, emotional, scholastic and behavioral functioning ... and that the majority (of the graduates) remember their stay at Orr Shalom as an important and positive experience in their lives" (Weiner, Fall 1990, 3).

In our own United States, there have been attempts to use such models, sometimes even to the extent of preserving the families in which abuse has taken place. In May 1991, a CBS short special filmed social workers daily helping families to stay together after abuse had occurred. In Maryland, three months of help at a cost of $1,000 to the society could save some children's family lives. Otherwise they would have been institutionalized or handed over to foster parents at a $10,000 cost for a short time period. Although three months has been proven to be not long enough to rehabilitate children's lives in a relatively healthy environmment, to the degree it would help would be a sure step in the right direction.

Orr Shalom had literally pulled children in chaos out of the streets and homes of abuse, as had Youth Aliyah's Kibbutz Rehabilitation Program and Three Rivers Youth's A.E.V.P. Other concepts of rehabilitation have been added by Three Rivers Youth; by wonderful new special work projects at city malls where at-risk youth can work, receive tutoring, and have a snack; and by various Big Brothers and Sisters and other caring mentoring programs in many states in this country. Hundreds of people have been trying for years to solve our youth's problems with scarce resources. These programs and others, such as the boy's ranches in Oklahoma, Texas, and western Pennsylvania, do attempt to prevent young boys and girls from reaching the streets of crime. In our cities, however, we still find one out of four youth who are high-risk, and one out of two who are at "normal-risk." Unless the very good programs are expanded and positive concepts are promoted to develop new projects, many more children will become at-risk, and our society will itself risk a loss in a major war against despair and crime.

As we face the 1990s, this battle must become a priority. In the last year, a new summer school program in New Orleans, named Desire, managed to keep young children out of the streets of a slum neighborhood. Although $900,000 in local and federal funds was spent on the school program during the summer months, the third and fifth graders' academic test results were not at all impressive. Since additional health and emotional problems that accompany the students to school for the extra summer months affect test scores, study habits and students' abilities to function in general, the program's coordinators and teachers understood that "everything does originate in the home."   "How can they envision themselves leaving Desire?" a fifth grade teacher asked rhetorically. "The masses don't escape" (Cooper, July 11, 1991, 13). During a summer program of only a few months duration, children return to their homes every evening, and in the long run, the impact on achievement cannot be certain. There is still much doubt whether such short programs in poor environments can change attitudes and skills and allow youth to escape such neighborhoods as Desire's.

Fifteen years ago, I used the term "high-risk youth" sparingly since it was not well-known then among American scholars. In the 1990s, however, this term is being used as often as <u>social problem</u>, <u>alcoholism</u>, <u>drug addiction</u>, <u>hunger</u>, and the <u>divorce rate</u>. We are now beginning to feel the effects of neglecting those problems and others among our thirty million poor people and dysfunctional families.

In the near future, it will not be enough to give a few hours of volunteer time to neighborhood watches, a trip to the food bank, or talking about liberal causes every few years. The federal, state and municipal governments need to invest monies, time, research, and professional manpower in innovative alternative educational programs in every city and state in our country. These programs must be established in supporting communities and be advanced, not blocked, by the bureaucracies of self-serving politicians who control purse strings.

First of all, highly trained professionals, such as educational directors, counselors, social workers, special education teachers, and psychologists must be hired to organize and work directly with our children, and, when still possible, their parents as well. Once such excellent educational people are in place, we can begin to create the most successful programs using models such as Youth Aliyah's Rehabilitation Program to turn the tide in the United States. There are many years of work ahead of us.

4
Integration of At-Risk Youth: Israeli Success with Youth Aliyah Programs

... do not save time but lose it.

Jean-Jacques Rosseau

THE SOCIAL GAP IN ISRAEL

In the early 1970s, Israeli educators, social workers, and scholars began to seek ways to create changes in the behavior patterns and political power structure of Israeli society. They
believed that through educational and social reforms, the mobility and status of Eastern youth and even a segment of the older
offspring of the "Desert Generation," whose core group immi-
grated to Israel in the 1950s from North Africa, would improve
over the next generation.

By the 1970s, it had become obvious that the modern Jewish
problem, lack of consensus in a pluralistic society, was the
pressing one which required an immediate solution. Social
integration was viewed as a means to strengthen the democratic
institutions of the young Israeli state, since assimilation and
acculturation had not yet succeeded. In university courses in
Israel, as well as in the United States, this theme was used as a
rationale for the study of the problem of Jewish integration in
Israel even before studying the Arab-Jewish problem. In the
1981 elections, this was borne out again when racial verbiage
and even violence spilled over into the streets or occurred at

political meetings, at Labor Party headquarters near Tel Aviv, and even at private homes and farms. Much of this antidemocratic behavior had roots in modern Israeli political history, as politicians admitted, but this time it occurred for ethnic and social reasons as well. Racist-like slogans and actions based on social-economic factors outdid the older political jealousies and rivalries of the pioneer days. Justice Chaim Landau recognized this and expressed it in April 1982 when he discussed his fears of the growing violence in Israeli society, as did the deputy president of the Association for Civil Rights in Israel (A.C.R.I.), Justice Chaim Cohen, who investigated charges of discrimination and violent treatment of the Israeli minorities.

Early in the same year, while attending a student seminar for activist students of Eastern Jewish origins, I heard angry tones expressing complaints about fruitless discussion and the lack of clear activist Sephardic goals and ways to achieve them in Israel. There was sharp criticism of the inequality in Israeli society from the audience, as well as from S. Sverski and A. Kedran, two scholars whose writings and experiences in the field of integration in Israel are well documented. The latter expressed many views based on his extensive work experiences and involvement in social activities in the poor Tikvah Quarter neighborhood of South Tel Aviv where he was living at that time. The dynamics of the meeting and the clear thrust of the participants' attitudes toward the problem's intensity helped me to understand the need for the State of Israel to find solutions in the immediate future.

The long-term goal of such a unique program as the Youth Aliyah Rehabilitation Program in Kibbutz was to assist the poor, disadvantaged youth of Eastern Jewish origin to become constructive citizens and to integrate them into a pluralistic society. In order to help close the social gap and integrate the Eastern Jewish youth into such an Israeli society, many programs and reforms must continually be initiated and evaluated; the policymakers will have to decide which ones can most benefit the society in the future.

Finally, after much research and experience, it was my view that in a highly supportive setting, as the kibbutz, a long-range educational program could succeed in achieving the goal of rehabilitation and could bridge the social gap between disadvantaged Eastern Israeli youth and Western Israeli youth. In other societies in the West, democratic organization and highly committed staffs can also achieve similar rehabilitation goals if the supportive environment and peer group approach exist and are utilized. As I have outlined so far in this book, various American programs are initiating unique peer group methods in order to further such processes in the appropriate environments. It is hoped that agencies and staffs will receive the resources to achieve some of their goals in the near future.

YOUTH ALIYAH AND ITS RESPONSES TO SOCIETAL NEEDS IN ISRAEL

The residential educational programs of Youth Aliyah were never isolated from the needs of the surrounding environment. All of Youth Aliyah's programs were organized to meet the immediate needs of certain segments of Israeli society and were viewed as attempts to achieve intermediate goals on the path toward a higher purpose. The sponsoring organization was highly dependent on and sensitive to streams of information that induced it to shift previous intermediate goals and develop new objectives.

The original goal of Youth Aliyah was to rescue Jewish children from war-torn Europe, and after the defeat of Nazi Germany it continued to help the Jewish children who survived the Holocaust. At this point, the environmental expression of need created a response of rehabilitation, of education, and of the striving toward social integration in the Jewish Yishuv (see Glossary) in Palestine. As history verifies, "15,000 youngsters were so saved and absorbed."

After the State of Israel was proclaimed, Zionist underground activities began to aid Jewish youngsters in escaping from Arab North African countries such as Morocco, Tunisia, Algeria, and Libya. These youngsters were also absorbed in kibbutzim (see Glossary), or newer youth villages. This social necessity to bring large numbers of youngsters from North Africa had to be met, and the task of absorbing them in Israel without their parents fell on the shoulders of Youth Aliyah. The essential goal of the "rescue operation" was their social integration in a Jewish homeland and the creation of a melting pot in the infant state.

In the following period (1956–1967), new educational institutions and new forms of rehabilitation were used, but the goal was basically still the same: to socially absorb chilren who needed some type of educational and social assistance. From 1967 to 1972, Youth Aliyah began again to shift its intermediate goals. The aim became the absorption of Russian Jews and Western Jews so that assimilation in communist and capitalist countries would not deplete the ranks of the Jewish people. The rescue of the remaining youth from North Africa and the Middle East countries also continued. Many of these children would come to Israel alone or with parents who could not help them integrate.

Finally, the last stage began, as Youth Aliyah became aware of its new obligations to integrate youth from urban "welfare dependency" families of Israel. Therefore, the rescuing of children, whose parents were killed or remained abroad, the educating of new immigrant children and rehabilitating socially maladjusted Israeli youth all represented intermediate goals toward which Youth Aliyah shifted. Yet all of these goals pointed toward the higher purpose of social integration. These stages, clearly defined by Chanoch Rinnot in Immigration and Settlement, included: (1) shifting intermediate goals stimulated by the needs of the environment within the Jewish Yishuv of pre-State Palestine; (2) the war-torn European situation; (3) the conditions of Jewish life in North Africa, the West, and the Soviet Union; and (4) in general, the policies of the authorities in Israel from 1948 to 1972. On July 7, 1972, there were 9,971 boys and girls being educated by Youth Aliyah, 8,376 in residential settings and 1,595 receiving whole-day vocational education at Youth Day Centers. On July 7, 1973, therer were 11,573 boys and girls being educated by Youth Aliyah, 9,791 in residential settings (Rinnot, 1973, 70–89).

Within one year, the Youth Aliyah population grew by 1,600, and in 1973–1974 it was to reach 12,500–13,000, according to Joseph Klarman, writing in the Israel Year Book of 1974. The director of the Children and Youth Aliyah Department of the Jewish Agency also added that from 1972 to 1973, there were 500 new children being admitted to kibbutzim, youth villages, or centers—some form of residential setting, where the "disadvantaged Israeli children" were cared for according to the new program.

AN OUTLINE OF THE RESEARCH PROPOSITIONS OF THE STUDY

I have formulated propositions which were designed to specifically analyze the outcomes of a Youth Aliyah peer group approach that was used within an educational program. The program attempted to fulfill specified socialization goals. The analysis was accomplished by comparing three groups in Israel:

(1) the Ramat Hakovesh Kibbutz Program group whose participants originated in the slums of Tel Aviv-Jaffa and who were school dropouts, a type of group which could be expected to be in trouble with the law;
(2) the South Tel Aviv group, an equivalent group to the Ramat Hakovesh Kibbutz Program group whose members also lived in the slums of Tel Aviv and who did not receive any program treatment before their army service;
(3) the youth movement group from the Negev development town of Sderot, whose members were equivalent in age and sex to the other two groups, but not in the socioeconomic status, and whose members had been organized during their high school period by a part-time madrich (see Glossary).

These three groups were compared in a research study, which began in 1977 when they entered the Israeli Army, on the basis of their national service experience and performance, their attitudes toward public service and social integration, and the degree of social adjustment which they made after the 1977 period, i.e., after the Ramat Hakovesh Rehabilitation Program had ended. The major proposition was stated as follows: "Peer group discipline and cooperation and the eventual cohesiveness of the chevrat noar (see Glossary), under close supervision of a madrich, in a highly idealistic and supportive environment can achieve socialization goals." My assumption was that the fact that the peer group structure and the nonformal educational methods used successfully by Youth Aliyah in the 1950s and 1960s were used in programs such as the Kibbutz Remedial Program at Ramat Hakovesh, and that this residential program lasted for a much longer period than the American encampment programs in the 1950s and 1970s would prove the above proposition true in the long run. My second proposition was formulated on the basis that the majority of these youngsters joined the Israeli Army's Nachal (see Glossary) organization at the end of their prolonged educational program. "The youth community would develop highly motivated youngsters who would have a high level of commitment to national (public) service." The Nachal sends its recruits to border areas to serve as a unit during an extended period of their service, and an additional time is spent on a kibbutz which, upon army completion, may become their collective home.

In addition, these facts led me to believe that the original youth community would include highly idealistic and motivated youngsters at the end of the program on a kibbutz. The second basic reason that the second proposition was formulated before the actual research began was that the cooperative lifestyle and Israeli youth movement type of education which the youngsters received during the two-year program on the kibbutz intensified their motivation to commit themselves to national service after they completed the two-year kibbutz program.

Various studies on integration of North African youth in Israel proved that there were positive effects on the attitudes of young people toward social integration if they had been members of youth movements in North Africa and Israel. These young people also had a high commitment toward public service in the State of Israel. An operational definition of public service can be found in Appendix II. Therefore, the second assumption for formulating the proposition will also hold true for those who did not join a <u>Nachal</u> unit, as well as for those who did join and who planned to return to the kibbutz as a part of a nucleus group after their army service. Finally, it was possible to find documentation that youth who join the <u>Nachal</u> express the attitude that they prefer voluntary-type work under hardship conditions to all other forms of service. This idealistic type of service had included only 10 to 15% of all Israeli youth as the 1970s came to a close. The fact that the <u>Nachal</u> includes within its general approach values that easily lend themselves to the fulfillment of public service tasks reinforces the second basic reason for formulating the related proposition which was expressed in this section and the rationale of which was herein reviewed.

In general, the staff of the Youth Aliyah Kibbutz Program include <u>madrichim</u> (see Glossary) and <u>metaplot</u> (see Glossary), as well as professional teachers, social workers, educational advisors recommended by the Ministry of Education, psychologists, supervisors, administrators, and clerical workers. In the Rehabilitation Program at Kibbutz Ramat Hakovesh, the <u>madrich</u> played the dominant social role in that he dealt with the individual level of treatment once the youngster reached the kibbutz. The <u>madrich,</u> Yitzchak Cohen, combined the functions of teacher, youth leader, and instructor. He was also selected on the basis of his experience as a youth leader and because of his personality traits, which marked him as a person suitable to counsel youth. He was a friend and guide of the youth as well as the supreme authority for the group once it arrived on the kibbutz. He also represented the kibbutz and its values to the adolescents and acted as the interpreter of this new way of life. He answered questions openly on an informal and formal level and from him I learned a great deal about the youth, the peer group-based educational methods, and the history of the program at Ramat Hakovesh.

The individual level of treatment, however, actually began with the first contact of the social worker of the municipality with whom urban candidates were in contact. The contact was continued by the social worker, Aaron Sharon, when the young-

ster first joined the group at the kibbutz and occurred throughout the period of adjustment and the group's unification. Its
intensity increased during the final stage when general planning
for the group's future was occurring. This process was explained and documented by Aaron, who also described the
follow-up period after 1977 and the statistical results, as well as
the group's relationship to the kibbutz after the army period.

The social worker only intervened when requested to do so
by the madrich who was responsible for the day-to-day care of
the individual and the group. Yitzchak Cohen, the madrich at
Ramat Hakovesh, had the major task to mold the individual
(with all his or her initial social problems) into becoming part of
the strongly self-disciplining and cohesive group, and to develop
within the group, through the interaction of committees, the
ability to cope with its own social problems, to create positive
recreational activities, and to form a healthy relationship with
the kibbutz.

The Youth Aliyah supervisor was the person who was
responsible for all the educational programs, whether they be
formal learning ones, informal meetings with other Youth
Aliyah groups, or discussion within the group about the future
of the participants in the army and in the kibbutz. The supervisor of the Kibbutz Remedial Program was usually responsible
for other Youth Aliyah programs in the area and was able to
evaluate progress being made in the educational realms of one
type of program compared to other types. In the kibbutz
program, known as the Kibbutz Remedial Program for youths
aged 16 to 18, the kibbutz provided one full-time professional
teacher, who was under the supervision of the Youth Aliyah
supervisor in terms of the formal education of the group.

The teacher of the Kibbutz Remedial Program, Hadas,
taught the youngsters a number of school subjects during an
early morning daily program of two hours of formal learning.
The curriculum of the learning program, as mentioned earlier,
was revised to meet the needs of the students who failed in their
previous school experiences. The teacher, a member of the
kibbutz, was an integral part of the staff, together with the
madrich, who was also a kibbutz member. The third member of

the internal staff was the <u>metapelet</u> (see Glossary), the house-mother, who was responsible for cleanliness, health care, and other more "motherly" concerns. The teacher related to the students on the social level as well as the formal educational level, since, other than the <u>madrich,</u> she was the only adult who met and worked with the group intensely on a day-to-day basis. The teacher and the <u>madrich</u> were, therefore, the major educators of the group and set the tone of the approach taken toward the group. Hadas provided me with candid opinions about the program, the methods the staff used, and the academic and social results. Her aid in the research was valuable, since she was frank about all aspects of the program she described.

In general, the staff organized all the formal educational and social activities within the kibbutz. They also had contact with the families of the young participants and all other institutions with which the group and its individuals related. Most of this contact was outside the kibbutz, and therefore the social worker was in the best position to carry out most of these tasks. The <u>madrich,</u> however, also maintained contact with the group while it was in the army. The housemother, too, related to the youngsters on a personal level and at times was the intermediary between them and the <u>madrich</u> regarding any personal problems which the young participants faced during the two years. Before I tried to make an analysis, the research propositions, the contacts with the kibbutz, and the youngsters who participated in the Ramat Hakovesh Program were first discussed with various staff members of the program itself. Their interest in objective research and their overall assistance were all necessary components of my project.

In deciding to do research on the Kibbutz Rehabilitation Program of Youth Aliyah, I was aware that some comparisons to both similar and different types of groups had to be made in order to create a valid study. Therefore, the group of development town youth of equivalent age, sex, and even neighborhood background was chosen, although their socioeconomic status and achievement levels in school were higher. This twelfth grade group which was a <u>garin</u> and did plan to join the <u>Nachal</u> as one unit, had grown up together in a youth movement and, as individuals, had strong leadership tendencies. Their goal was to become a nucleus group which later would settle in kibbutz. The older group was the loose street gang, one without any guidance or distinct youth program. It frequented the Barbour Center in South Tel Aviv and was equivalent in age, sex, socio-economic status, and school achievement to the participants at Ramat Hakovesh.

The random sample from South Tel Aviv was chosen from a total population of street gangs who roamed around the Barbour Center. Occasionally, this group participated in nonformal activities, but never was there an "active" membership unit which was a constant source of friction between the coordinators in the center and "the gang." Having had some direct contact with them and their soccer coach who worked at the Barbour Center in 1977, I was able to speak to them as individuals and interview them, their friends, and relatives during the years 1977–1980. All of them lived in the famous Tikvah Quarter, in Neve Tzahal, Yad Eliyahu, or Kefar Shalem, neighborhoods which were in close proximity to the Barbour Center. All of them were approaching eighteen in 1977.

The Ramat Hakovesh group was chosen after a number of discussions with a Youth Aliyah supervisor and Aaron Sharon, a social worker of the Tel Aviv Municipality. It consisted of young people from lower-class neighborhoods in South Tel Aviv and Jaffa whose families were welfare cases. The youngsters from these areas had difficulties remaining in school and at work. In this case, two municipal social workers were given overall responsibility for supervising and advising the kibbutz counselors and teachers at Ramat Hakovesh. They played a very important role in the Ramat Hakovesh program and similar ones in the area. It was with the help of one of the social workers that I made contact with the Ramat Hakovesh program participants. The formal visits to this group at the kibbutz were also done with the cooperation of the madrich and the teacher and occurred at least a dozen different times over the two-and-a-half-year period. It was during these visits that questionnaires were filled out and some interviews took place.

At a number of these visits, I ate lunch in the kibbutz dining room with individuals of the group, saw their rooms, discussed their experiences in the kibbutz program, and relaxed in the kibbutz clubhouse with them. As a kibbutz member myself, I felt relaxed in these situations, not as an urban middle-class professional might feel. At times, I met small groups in their rooms and had meetings with them outside the kibbutz. These formal and informal visits took place during their vacations from the army, as well as just before they entered the service and upon their completion of it as well. I saw them growing in confidence each time that I visited them.

The group from the development town of Sderot was also selected in 1977 through a working contact with one of ten original youth members. The participants had formally established a framework for a Nachal garin and intended to serve part of their service in the Negev kibbutz of Grofit.

The development town sample (Sderot has a population of 8,000 people and never developed industry or adequate services) was purposely selected as a balance between the "street gang" group which did not have any program and the unique educational program at Ramat Hakovesh. Kibbutz Ramat Hakovesh was of the Meuchad movement, ideologically in the center in relationship to the other two kibbutz movements. As the 1970s came to a close, it united with its more conservative ideological partner of the past to form the new Tnua Hakibbutzit Hameuchedet or T.A.K.A.M.

There was a certain similarity between the Sderot sample and the Ramat Hakovesh population due to the youth movement educational program which the former group experienced; yet the lack of a long residential program created differences and did not allow similarities to develop. On the other hand, this lower-middle-class and middle-class youth population of Sderot was very different from the South Tel Aviv street gang population. The first meeting with them was at the clubhouse of the Pioneer Women (Working Women's Club), where a parent with whom I had made contact was the coordinator. Later, each individual together with his/her parents and many sisters and brothers were interviewed at home. Their twelfth grade homeroom teacher and the vice-principal of the high school also cooperated in the initial stages.

Although the case study approach I used was limited in generalizability because of the dependence on a single instance, it partially overcame this limitation through a repeated use of measurements which have been applied under similar circumstances. The repeated use of common measures helped to build up a body of knowledge as well as validate the statistical results. The comparison between outcomes of similar programs can aid other evaluators in assessing the effectiveness of various programs, as was one of the ultimate goals of my study within its own framework. Finally, in devising measures which would test the effectiveness of a program on a longer range basis than the average, I attempted to analyze a number of variables which would enable me to trace an outcome at the end of a few years. In such a framework, a long-range in-depth study, the measures were changing as the subjects' lifestyle changed.

Although the basic independent variable, the program, remained a stable element, its effect on participants' attitudes toward social integration could be effectively measured only if a long-range study were used to analyze possible changing outcomes. Proximate measures taken soon after similar educational programs had not proved a relationship between the short- and long-range goals of such programs. Hyman and Wright's analysis of short-range programs' outcome verified this point. Their claim was that the ability to measure the outcomes of a short-range program effectively was hindered by the fact that the sentiments of young people are not in themselves evidence of the effectiveness of short-range programs; but if programs could be extended, one could measure their effectiveness after completion and for a number of subsequent years. It was this latter view that seemed logical, and its results proved that a new approach was needed.

When analyzing attitudes toward integration, a number of points must be discussed which relate specifically to carrying out a valid study of a peer group program which sought changes in behavior and attitudes toward social integration. For instance, how many things must people do together to be considered integrated? How persistently must they continue to do these common tasks? There are a number of models by which to measure the degree of integration of any one group. Jacob and Teune named at least ten factors which might exert integrative influence on people. Some of them are: transactions or interactions among people and groups, geographic proximity, homogeneity, and previous integrative experiences (Jacob and Teune, 1964, 11–12).

There were elements of a number of these factors which became apparent when I interviewed the participants. For example, if my questions related to personal contact during worktime, or to style or leisure between the various ethnic and class groups of the country, the answers could signify transactions and interactions (personal contact) which could lead to a more positive attitude toward other ethnic and class groups on the part of the lower class Eastern Israeli youth. This could eventually lead to their overall better adjustment to Israeli society. Finally, the element of geographic proximity was always being considered when attitude questions were asked and when the teachers, counselors, and social workers were being interviewed by me.

In order to collect the data on the influence of the Kibbutz Remedial Program on attitudes toward social integration, I formulated a number of attitude questionnaires (Appendix III). One was used shortly after the program was completed (six weeks after its official ending), and the other during the middle of the army service. A third questionnaire which dealt with public service was also applied toward the end of the army service (Appendix IV). There were a number of behavioral checklists administered to teachers, counselors, parents and friends—in general, the "human judges" who knew the young people personally and verified characteristic qualities and tendencies which the answers to the questionnaires manifested. Reliability was rechecked by using acceptable research methods.

The last set of questionnaires was administered to the Tel Aviv counselors and focused on two major areas of interest: the influence of the various programs on the attitudes of the youth in regard to the goal of social integration, and the behavioral

outcomes as a result of the programs. The results of this set of
questionnaires were proven to be reliable on the basis of the
well-known Spearman Brown Split Half Test (Table A.1). The
behavioral characteristics which were analyzed were based on
the checklists used by Youth Aliyah social workers before and
after the youth entered the program. For this reason, it was
possible to collect data on the youth of the Ramat Hakovesh
Rehabilitation Program from 1975–1977 and to compare the
differences between behavioral characteristics during the <u>Kelet</u>
period and towards the end of the two-year <u>Hachshara Hatzira</u>
program. This long-range analysis was the direct means to
carry out the study plan in order to have a valid analysis of
changing attitudes and behavioral patterns of young participants in a unique educational rehabilitation program.

Other information about the program and its outcomes was
gathered during interviews with the social worker of the Tel
Aviv Municipality, the Youth Aliyah supervisor, and the Barbour Center coordinator. These interviews were scheduled in
order to provide more background information about the
Youth Aliyah Program on a kibbutz and the need for special
social and educational programs in community centers in Israel.

THE EDUCATIONAL PROCESS IN KIBBUTZ
REHABILITATION PROGRAMS

The educational setting which Youth Aliyah had established
within veteran <u>kibbutzim</u> and youth villages was organized to
help create "the new Israeli culture" out of many different
ethnic Jewish groups which were emigrating from North Africa,
Western Europe, Australia, the Middle East, the Americas, and
Canada. As outlined in the Introduction, the educational
process within the residential settings is of specific interest to
professional educators who see the need to work with "disadvantaged" or "deprived" youth in the United States or in the
developing countries of the world. Youth Aliyah's aims have
never been merely instruction and physical welfare, but education in the widest sense of the term so that "the child would find

his place and play his part in the new society" (Rinnot, 1973, 81).

The kibbutz was seen as an instrument of education in the early 1970s, as in the past, superior to any other educational framework outside the family. As opposed to life in a children's home or a children's village, education is given not on an island separated from the life of an adult society, but as an organic part of the society to which children and adults both belong. The kibbutz, in particular, was seen as the only sector in Israel's society where the new immigrants, and in the case of Youth Aliyah's goals, immigrant children from European as well as Eastern countries, were really integrated and lived together in close community with the oldtimers and their children. There alone—perhaps with the exception of the army—the expression, Kibbutz Galiyot (the Ingathering of the Exiles) had real meaning.

To integrate the children into the social fabric of the new environment and at the same time give them individual attention, Youth Aliyah utilized two distinctive instruments: the chevrat noar and the madrich. The chevrat noar was the characteristic unit comprised of about forty young people of similar ethnic groups who stayed together for two to four years. The unit might have been attached to a kibbutz which thus became an educational settlement or became part of a youth village or another educational institution run by Youth Aliyah. The chevrat noar in a kibbutz was and still is today an educational framework complete in itself; i.e. it is not part of any other institution or school, even if contact with other peer groups is kept. It therefore has no model to emulate, no precedent except previous chevrot noar to lean upon, and no actual standard of comparison by which to judge itself.

The dynamic development through which the Youth Aliyah rehabilitation peer group passes is different from the dynamic development of all other peer groups on the kibbutz and within the framework of chevrat noar on kibbutzim. In the first stage of its development, the madrich has to show initiative and flexibility, since in that stage, more than in any other, the group is a separate closed unit. It is at this stage that the madrich is the person upon whom the group is highly dependent, until in the later stages (after six months most groups enter the second stage), the adolescents gain experience and self-confidence, and their initiatives and creative energies are sufficiently aroused to enable them to act with an ever-increasing degree of independence. The first stage is referred to as "individual adjustment," the second stage "formation of the group," and the third stage "integration."

> In the second stage, there are a number of internal crises, as conflicts over leadership arise; but by the end of this stormy period, the group is united and has set up permanent institutions of a democratic and egalitarian nature. During the third stage, the peer group is widened to its extreme boundaries and the days of blossoming begin. The group by this time (usually the last six months of the program) gathers force to prepare to handle its future tasks. The group is ready to create an independent society (Ritter, 1973, 3).

As the group develops in stages, the youngsters are passing through dynamic periods of development. In the first half of the second year, which is considered the quietest and most fruitful period of all, each individual arrives at a new self-evaluation. During this period of group formation, a new social consciousness is created. Now the adolescents have settled down in an agricultural branch and are learning it thoroughly. In this last stage, they are interested in the current affairs of the kibbutz, while at school they are learning new subjects. Social activity is regulated and intense. As the group establishes bonds with youth movements in the country, the members do become interested in local and national, social, and political questions. However, the group has not yet begun serious discussions about the future.

As the second year comes to a close, the future occupies the minds of the young people. Social activity reaches its zenith. Committee work is intense and increasingly independent. The madrich dares not press the youngsters into decisive discussions. He must allow them to arrive freely at the point of self-searching and decision. The number of youth that remain in the nucleus form a garin which, in regard to Youth Aliyah's programs of the 1970s, has as its goal joining the mother kibbutz after their army service. As in the past, the ideology was based purely on the pioneering idea. After the two-year programs were completed, the nucleus group either stayed a third year working on the mother kibbutz, united with older kibbutzim, or lived in villages and worked as hired labor until the Jewish National Fund allotted them land on which to settle as an original garin. At times they joined a young kibbutz which had not yet received its full complement of members. In the 1970s, however, the army period was divided between basic training, service in the kibbutz as part of the Israeli Army's Nachal program, and the unique goal of returning to the kibbutz as members of the garin and the settlement itself.

Youth Aliyah today does not view as a failure any number of possibilities, such as some of the graduates of the program joining a separate army unit from that of the garin and/or returning to their original neighborhoods, or any other rural or urban settlement other than the kibbutz. In this case, the goal of social integration has not necessarily replaced the long-range goal of the earlier period, but it clearly plays a more dominant role than the previous pioneering goals of the 1940-1960s.

The goal of the educational program at Ramat Hakovesh was explicitly to rehabilitate and prepare a group of disadvantaged Sephardic Jewish youth to be constructive citizens in society. The group was to be absorbed into the kibbutz in 1975 and remain there until 1977 when their army service began. It was written and stated at various times that breaking the "welfare cycle" of family and neighborhood, even if the subjects did not settle in the kibbutz after their army service, was the goal set by the Youth Aliyah supervisor, the madrich, the teacher, the housemother, as well as the kibbutz members, and the social workers of the Tel Aviv Municipality. From their point of view, the group that joined the Nachal and even considered remaining as a garin to Ramat Hakovesh after their army service was over succeeded.

The program's foremost success was that all of the nineteen members (of the original twenty-one participants) who remained after the initial six months finished the program, and some had become socially integrated into the kibbutz even before they had joined the Nachal. Also, eleven finished the Nachal, together remaining a garin which was considered a relatively high number for even such an educational program as this one.

The social integration of many of the youth was indicated by the social worker, Aaron Sharon, who pointed out that the participants were truly adopted by the families, that their participation in day-to-day kibbutz activities became normal procedure, and that the relationships that eventually developed at work and with the equivalent age youth of the kibbutz were major factors in their integration on kibbutz. The early preparation of most of the youth and the accompanying care of the workers and the Youth Aliyah supervisor helped the program to succeed in achieving its goals. The other major factor that helped the peer group program to succeed was the early crystallization of the group by performing group activities within the first two months of their arrival. These types of social activities can be used in a similar fashion by all peer group managed programs for-high risk youth and have been done so recently with positive outcomes according to coordinators with whom I have spoken.

However, the force de major in the early successes of such a strong educational peer group program was the madrich's role as the dominant personality that molded the group at Ramat Hakovesh. This type of strong personality is a necessity in similar programs in both Israel and America—the youth model who leads the way. The madrich kept the group together from the beginning of the program until the end. Although on a gradual basis he allowed various committees to function, and the membership social committee clarified problems on social situations toward the end of the two-year period, it was Yitzchak who kept the participants together in a forceful way. He allowed them to organize their cultural activities at the beginning and to develop relationships at work and with their adopting families.

However, regarding their general kibbutz interactions on a day-to-day basis and their individual and group behavior, he was the responsible adult model.

At its inception, the program included two hours of study, six hours of work and group and individual activities, and discussions organized by the madrich. After a short orientation period, families adopted the young participants and began to invite them for four o'clock tea hour. As the youngsters gained more responsibility at work and the group developed socially as well as academically, contacts were made with the youth of the kibbutz. Most of the youngsters felt that this two-year program did develop their personalities, their work abilities, and their intellectual prowess to a great extent; the relationships at work, the formal studies, which included a special curriculum managed by Hadas under the supervision of the Youth Aliyah supervisor, and those more frequent opportunities to meet with youngsters from the kibbutz were all aspects which would help the participants become constructive citizens of Israel.

The democratic organization of the group into committees, and their encouragement by the staff after the first six months are two aspects of the program which later would help the participants to develop friends from other social and ethnic groups. As mentioned above, the staff used the carrot-and-stick method in class and in the social area as well, but the madrich created the force which developed self-control while still allowing the democratic committee system to organize and clarify rules during the second half of the program.

In the study program, basic reading, math, and language were taught, as well as sports and other extracurricular interests. This special type of curriculum is used where necessary in all Youth Aliyah programs. In general, however, each student advanced at his or her own level in the various subjects and was constantly encouraged to find his or her own area of interest. Hadas stressed that although she felt two hours of study was not long enough to close the achievement gap, there was general improvement in the academic field, especially in writing skills, spelling, expression, and cognitive abilities. In other programs, not on a kibbutz, study is the major emphasis for a period of time and later, more work time is given as the academic goals are reached. Hadas was able to give at least eight examples of participants who progressed academically, most of whom were from the eleven garin members who stayed in the Nachal until the end of their army service. When asked about their ability to compete with Western Israelis, she felt most of the nineteen participants still had a way to go to catch up, but in a few cases the gap was small. She felt that two or three of the eight who had shown great academic improvement would get along well in middle-class Israeli urban society. Three or four participants were positive leaders in the classroom and in social situations.

Although there were some "trouble makers" at the beginning of the program, she felt most of them had advanced as students and had worked out most of their personal problems. She gave some credit to the peer group pressure exerted, the madrich's influence, and her own carrot-and-stick method. In general, the staff attempted to fulfill the function of a "normal family" substitute for the young participants, and the addition of family adoptions played a large role in the nonformal aspect of the educational program. The family involved had to be supervised and counseled so as to develop a good relationship with the participant; there is no doubt that this was one of the great contributing factors to the educational program's success.

The program did generally succeed in achieving its goals in all of the major fields examined, including behavioral patterns which showed steady improvement from the time of the Kelet preparation period until the end of the program in 1977. The characteristics studied were based on original Youth Aliyah lists devised by the social workers of that agency. The differences distinguished were easy to draw out and analyze, and, as in other areas, were extremely clear in regard to the high level achieved by the Ramat Hakovesh participants. The educational program emphasized: relationship to work, to learning, and to the authority of staff members; acceptance of responsibility; emotional stability; social position in the group; social adjustment; and outward appearance.

In the educational diagnosis of the youths' behavior, all of them succeeded in receiving good marks from their teacher and madrich, again proving that the staff felt specific behavioral changes were accomplished by the participants in the rehabili-

tation program. This analysis together with that of their ideological and public service attitudes and integration attitude
scores, all point the way to specific progress which the Ramat
Hakovesh program's participants did make, and this includes
closing the social and scholastic achievement gap between
disadvantaged Eastern Jewish youth and Western Israelis of
equivalent age in the cities and even in kibbutzim.

   When I compared the group of participants to the elite
garin from Sderot–all high school graduates who had studied
together, been in a youth movement together, and were form-
ing a Nachal garin together–the Ramat Hakovesh group still
was highly crystallized. This was achieved by many extra-curricular activities–hikes, sleep-outs, evening cultural activities,
holiday parties, and song-fests, all of which took place within
the first three months of the participants' arrival at the kibbutz.
However, the main feeling of "togetherness" occurred as the
group's own democratic peer group organization began to
function; the kibbutz assistance, especially in the area of family
adoption, work relationships, and the general positive feedback
from the kibbutz membership and institutions opened up new
horizons and affected their previous attitudes. ("We were
saving Jewish souls not exploiting anyone; and until 1978 we
were committed to take this group as a garin," said Hadas in an
interview in 1980.) It was soon obvious to the kibbutz and to
Yitzchak, the madrich, that this group was unique and could be
molded into a functioning democratic and mature garin to
kibbutz. Yitzchak admitted that it took every evening of individual and group discussions to build up the confidence that
they needed and to move them into the second and third stages
("formation of group" and "integration").

   The typical leadership conflicts occurred, as they set up
their democratic institutions, but even more problematic was
the later stage when the individuals had to make major decisions. Some of them decided to go their own way by joining
regular army or elite units outside the Nachal framwork (a good
number went through officer courses), and many became socially interested in the kibbutz and/or some particular young
person of its garin membership. As this happened, Yitzchak

and Aaron had to be especially sure that they did not pressure the participants to make decisions which fit the more idealistic goals of Youth Aliyah and the kibbutz. Many youngsters who did not join the Nachal did wish to remain in contact with the kibbutz, and in 1980 the young army men and women returned to work there, as customarily done by Nachal groups toward the end of their service. Even those who had not joined the Nachal returned on leaves to be with their peer group and friends and families at Ramat Hakovesh.

This period of "homecoming" was and is a key in all such programs, and each kibbutz's ability to absorb the soldiers depends on its organization and attitudes toward that garin. As of June 1980, Yitzchak's hard work had achieved some spectacular results as two girls married a serviceman and policeman who had high ranks, and they finished their service with good records. It is true that in juxtaposition to such "rehabilitation" and "integration" into Israeli society as constructive citizens, the army period put distance between the group and the kibbutz on a social level, and the madrich himself became somewhat disappointed in 1980 in its relationship to the youthful participants. However, the peer group had developed ideally through the stages whereby a garin of the Nachal had been formed, there was a high percentage of rehabilitation and good records in the army; the attitudes and behavioral patterns had reached a very high level in comparison to the Sderot and Barbour Center Groups, as well as in comparison to other groups of its own background.

In the beginning of the army service period, the young participants were rated highly by their officers in basic training. The close contacts maintained by Yitzchak and Aaron were generally a continuation of the educational process which had begun in 1975. As 1978 approached and the six-month period of the basic training ended, there were optimistic feelings about this group's unique qualities.

However, the group had left the highly supportive ideal community, and some of its social relationships with the outside world must have diminished its feelings of being a unique elite group. In reality, it was in competition with other Nachal groups with members from middle-class and upper-class Western families, and this took its toll on the garin members who were in Nachal, as well as Yitzchak himself, who once bitterly remarked that so-called higher intellectual groups in the army were looking down on his youth. Also, during this period the ties of the youth to the kibbutz institutions levelled off, and some participants felt that they were now just an added work force soon to return to the home base. The attitudes of the staff, however, remained warm and accepting, and the participants were constantly encouraged to fulfill their goals in the army. As mentioned above, 1980 saw the end of varied army careers—many trained officers, over 50 percent finishing the Nachal as a garin, and in all cases, good discipline records without one A.W.O.L. case, nor felonious crimes nor severe punishments listed for breaches of army discipline. There were good results on army performance and intelligence type tests as well (Table A.2).

Considering the background and the problems even during the two-year period at Ramat Hakovesh, it is remarkable how well the youngsters did from September 1977 until June 1980 when they finished their army service. Some of the young participants I met in that last year were certainly mature young men and women who had found direction. In this chapter, I will outline the results, with the figures on social and ideological attitudes and the behavioral patterns which changed from 1975 to 1980. It will be clear how the process of education in the army together with Yitzchak and Aaron's follow-ups and the support of the adopting families and kibbutz members enabled the program to affect them positively after 1977 as well. Aaron concluded in his last discussion with me in 1980 that the garin would not end up as one to Ramat Hakovesh because the kibbutz as a whole would not commit itself to accepting the group. Thus, the final ideological kibbutz act did not occur.

Consequently, this unique group of youngsters would have to integrate into society as individuals, which no one doubted they could do. The peer group models had achieved their goals, which were to create the necessary changes in order to help youth adjust socially and integrate into the general Israeli society. In fact, some of those youngsters might be found in other kibbutzim, in elite units of the permanent army, or in other public service positions, as they establish their professional goals and embark upon their careers in the state. It was not unusual in the past for high-ranking army officers, industrial and social leaders, and even some government officials to have spent a number of years during their youth in Youth Aliyah educational programs. This is well known by most of the Israeli population today, and the agency is highly valued within the society because of such achievements for the homeless and helpless youth with whom it worked.

THE RESULTS OF THE REHABILITATION PROGRAM AT RAMAT HAKOVESH

Most of the specific information gathered between 1977 and 1980 provided me with the statistical and general figures and description of results which were relevant to the analysis in this chapter. Most of the data was received from nineteen participants at Ramat Hakovesh, nine from the Barbour Center, and seven from the Sderot group, but certain attitudinal questionnaires were analyzed by examining only the nine members of the garin–members who remained in the Nachal unit together until the end of the service period. As to the Leisure Time Questionnaire, it was completed only by the Sderot and Ramat Hakovesh groups during the early period of the army service. The behavioral rating forms were filled out by the madrichim at meetings set up for this purpose, and the Behavioral Checklists were filled out by all the neighbors, friends, and subjects' relatives who answered the "yes"-"no" lists in their homes. The groups and subjects' friends and relatives usually cooperated, as did the Tel Aviv social workers, the Sderot homeroom teacher, the youth movement madrich, the Barbour madrich, and, of course, the staff at Ramat Hakovesh.

In many instances, questionnaires were filled out in group meetings, especially at Ramat Hakovesh and Sderot, where participants asked me to send them results or even "the research paper." In the case of the Barbour group, there was hesitation and even difficulty in locating the members and getting answers. This is consistent with the type of participants or nonparticipants that they were.

Information from the army came from a variety of sources including a commander, the _madrichim_ who visited the young soldiers at their bases, the Tel Aviv Social Work Department, and the Manpower Headquarters which did provide general information and some test results. Information regarding all nineteen Ramat Hakovesh participants was provided either from biographical files, follow-up work by the Tel Aviv Social Work Department, and from behavioral checklists of the _madrichim_ of the _Kelet_ (before the beginning of the program at Ramat Hakovesh, 1975), as well as the staff at Ramat Hakovesh after 1977.

One can never diminish the importance of the extensive legwork it takes to study such a unique educational program since running around (literally) through the Tikvah Quarter, the sandy paths of Kefar Shalem which separated a myriad of shacks, the narrow streets of Sderot, and the better known neighborhoods of Jaffa and Barbour Center's northern area all contributed to my understanding of how the participants had grown up and what families and environments had nourished them. It took a dozen or more such trips to each area to complete my study, and it is an experience I recommend to all researchers of the living conditions in the urban community of Tel Aviv or the Northern Negev development towns such as Sderot. It was a unique opportunity to carry out such intensive research with three different types of youth. The results were gathered from enough varied questionnaires and checklists used over long enough a period of time to be valid and help me to achieve the goal of my study plan.

In dividing the results on social integration, I concluded that there were three categories to measure the changing or lack of changing attitudes of the young participants in the various programs. The categories were: (1) attitudes toward social and ethnic groups other than one's own and relationships toward such other groups; (2) attitudes in terms of long-range relationships, i.e., friendships and places of residence; and (3) personal life situations and social integration. The results of Questionnaire A presented in Table A.3 outlines the results by depicting the averages of interval scores for all the groups on each of the above categories. In four cases, the Ramat Hakovesh group's lead was significant over the Sderot group, while in Section 1, especially, its scores were lower than that group.

When all the averages were taken, Ramat Hakovesh had relatively large point leads over the Barbour group, but also ranked behind this group a number of times. There was not an overall significant difference on this subject, as can be seen in Table A.3. When the behavioral checklists were analyzed, it was found that the correlations on isolated questions were high and reinforced the results in Section I. When questions from Sections II and III were also analyzed, they too correlated highly with the behavioral checklists. Although the results did not exhibit significant differences among the three groups, in attitudes toward long-range friendships and residence desires, the social integration scores of Ramat Hakovesh exhibited large leads over both of the groups. Ramat Hakovesh scored higher than the Sderot group on a willingness to marry people of other groups. However, on other questions concerning attitudes toward other ethnic groups, as well as parents' roles in accepting friends, its lead was high only over the Barbour subjects.

In the answers given by madrichim and the social coordinator, the Ramat Hakovesh and Sderot groups exhibited a more positive orientation toward future social integration. In summarizing the social integration results, therefore, present attitudes of Ramat Hakovesh participants were more positive than members of the other groups (Barbour and Sderot) on residence desires, attitudes toward different ethnic and social (class) groups, and the general future orientations toward social integration. This was only the first area of changed attitudes and behavioral patterns of Ramat Hakovesh participants that I was to discover as I analyzed their answers in comparison with the other two groups.

Another area which related to closing the social gap and which was examined was the social mobility of the participants.

Using a Leisure Time Questionnaire which presented separate questions on preferences for hobbies, music, reading, types of television programs viewed, and various social activities, including youth movement activities of an educational nature, I was able to discover another side to the personalities of the nine from Ramat Hakovesh and the seven from Sderot. The goal of this set of questions was to analyze tendencies toward upward social mobility of subjects who had participated in the residential program and had mixed with other classes and ethnic groups in comparison with the group which internally was at a higher class level and was more or less already integrated. One must add that the Sderot group was a movement group and its many youth movement activities were taken for granted (Table A.4).

The lack of any significant difference creates a definite impression that the two groups were similar in sociocultural leisure outlets after the summer of 1977. (The Sderot participants averaged eighty points and the Ramat Hakovesh group seventy.) In another test of social mobility, it was discovered that the Ramat Hakovesh kibbutz group exhibited a more positive orientation toward future professional careers, while having poor socioeconomic backgrounds (see Table A.5). Since the Ramat Hakovesh group never had opportunities to participate in many social activities which were socioeducational, it was natural for me to reach the conclusion that the Ramat Hakovesh Rehabilitation Program did change their sociocultural activity and their preferences; this can be seen as affecting its overall upward social mobility. This revelation was one of the major points which verified the change in the former slum participants.

When I reviewed the results of the major attitudinal questionnaire divided into public service commitment, ideology, and social adjustment, I took into account that only specific categories were chosen to be analyzed, and these were formed by scoring a question or clusters of questions which constituted such a category. There was a Zionist-oriented attitude questionnaire parallel to one of the categories dealing with ideology. Together, these two categories created an opportunity to affirm or negate the original proposition which related to a high commitment to national (public) service.

What was most interesting was that the analysis of the results of the ideological category showed little significant difference between the three groups. The results of these tests, however, showed Sderot and Ramat Hakovesh reacting similarly when choosing the "friendship" preference and the need to bring about harmony between parents and sons and daughters.

The last category, the Egotistical Category, showed little if any difference among the three groups. In terms of Part B, the Zionist orientation for each group was tested. It was examined as a feature of ideology. Since the Barbour group had only four members who participated, I decided not to try to gauge the significance of the group's average. In the case of the Ramat Hakovesh's group average, there was a tendency to reach the same level as the Sderot participant's average. For example, four of the former group's participants scored over the overall fifty-eight average and four under it; whereas the Sderot group had two over it and four under it. Again, the Zionist attitudes of the Ramat Hakovesh group was at least as positive as the Sderot group, although there were large and significant differences in background, including youth movement participation which connotes strong Zionist orientation. These results verified my initial assumptions that living in the highly idealistic Zionist atmosphere of a kibbutz strengthened the ideological and Zionist attitudes of the youth involved in such a unique educational program.

The Behavioral Characteristics Questionnaires were filled out in 1977 by the madrichim of the programs, except for the Ramat Hakovesh madrich's answers which were also filled out in 1975 during the Kelet period. The nine behavioral categories of which the last one was divided into three parts are based on the averages of points scored for all three groups and a comparison of the Ramat Hakovesh group's patterns between 1975 and 1977. The Sderot group's mean was 4.3. The Barbour group averaged 4.3, and the Ramat Hakovesh group had an average of 4.7 in 1977 and 3.7 in 1975 (Table A.6). When these averages were analyzed more in depth, in terms of the ranges of each group on various categories, there were the following results: In all cases except one, the Sderot group's range was relatively high in the learning motivation and unbridled sexual impulses categories. The lower ranges were in the characteristics such as lack of responsibility, attitudes toward authority, and emotional stability. The Ramat Hakovesh group had relatively few lower scores in the violence/unbridled sexual impulses characteristic syndrome. Most of the lower scores were in the areas of acceptance of responsibility, relationship to authority, status in social groups, and relationship to learning. The Barbour group's lower scores were in areas of unbridled sexual impulses, violence, emotional stability, relationship to authority, status in the social group, and responsibility.

In general, the findings showed that the Sderot and Barbour groups' weaknesses in the areas of violence and unbridled sexual impulses were similar, whereas the Ramat Hakovesh group scored highly. In the learning motivation, lack of responsibility, and attitude toward authority, the Sderot and Ramat Hakovesh groups overlapped. One can assume that if the Barbour group had been checked in 1978, it would have scored in the lower range in the above areas. Since I had the scores on behavioral patterns for the Ramat Hakovesh group in 1975, I was able to see that it scored as low as the other two groups did in 1977 in the violence and unbridled sexual impulse syndrome. It also had low scores in 1975 in those areas mentioned above where it had achieved the higher scores in 1977. The improvement included all the characteristics on which both Sderot and the Barbour groups had lower scores in 1977, i.e., the characteristics on which the scores for the Ramat Hakovesh group had been previously lower.

If one adds the reports of the Israeli Army officers, their teachers, and the social workers to the trend, one can easily identify a consistent improvement of the Ramat Hakovesh group in comparison with the Barbour group especially, which had a similar social background. For example, of the nine Ramat Hakovesh subjects, only one did not finish the Nachal service due to ill health, and he became a cook in the regular army unit. One went through an officer's course after receiving a high recommendation from the <u>Nachal</u> Command, and seven went smoothly through the <u>Nachal</u> service. Two of the seven were considered officer caliber. Of the Sderot group, four boys and girls finished the <u>Nachal</u> service. One other boy spent his army service in a development town as a <u>madrich</u> of youth movement groups. One was in an officer's course in 1980, and one was asked to join one. Of the Barbour group, one boy became a corporal in the Air Force, and two completed normal regular Israeli Army service. The other five boys had serious discipline or even criminal problems ranging from being A.W.O.L. to manslaughter accusations and trials at which a few were found to be guilty.

The results of the service records (Table A.2) can be compared to some of the levels of behavioral characteristics, such as "relationship to authority" and "lack of responsibility." In these areas and in general, progress was made by the Ramat Hakovesh group in the behavioral categories described in this section. During the army service period, the individuals from Barbour had to fend for themselves, and their individual and family problems led to negative reactions on the part of a majority. It is also clear from these results that rehabilitation programs have more effect upon the behavioral patterns of youth who originate in poorer environments than upon middle class youth, whose attitudes and behavioral patterns are changed by the development of a peer group educational approach and in programs such as the one at Ramat Hakovesh.

In the final analysis, the behavioral patterns and social achievement of the Ramat Hakovesh participants were on a par with the Sderot <u>garin</u>, allowing them to perform the same public service tasks in the army and in the long run, having the same positive attitudes and potential to do more in that area, as well as generally integrating into Israeli society.

These are the conclusions which I reached from the set of relevant findings I outlined in this chapter. It became obvious to me that long-term residential programs in idealistic and supportive environments and the use of a peer group educational approach do create change of attitudes toward social integration and behavioral patterns of welfare dependent and high-risk youth in Israel or in the West wherever such programs are instituted. The democratic type of organization within peer group-managed programs are important elements which must be allowed to flourish in order for the effects of such a unique method to be achieved in idealistic environments such as the kibbutz. Residential educational programs such as the one at Ramat Hakovesh can achieve social integration and close the social gap between poorer ethnic groups and middle-class groups which have come from better socioeconomic environments. Similar results can be achieved through such unique peer group educational programs as the one at Highfields, New Jersey, or an extended Three Rivers Youth A.E.V.P. in Pittsburgh, Pennsylvania, or in any other place where policymakers, educators, and social program initiators and administrators use their imaginations and evaluation skills to devise and perform the necessary act of administering such types of model programs as the one herein described and analyzed. Experience and research were the two aids which helped me reach the conclusions that there are similarities between the unique educational programs in the United States and Israel.

Before I summarize and provide an opportunity to the reader to reflect on some of the facts and ideas presented, I would like to add a few points about the personality of the Ramat Hakovesh group. As mentioned earlier, these young student-workers who grew as individuals to such a great extent in two years on the kibbutz did not have the lives of opportunity that most middle-class children do have. They learned to work as skilled technicians or highly trained workers in kibbutz industries and in the service branches, and they made great strides on a social level in a community which is very tightly knit, and usually critical of new people before they are absorbed. The participants of the Ramat Hakovesh Kibbutz Program, however, organized themselves into a highly cohesive youth society, while at the same time they learned to accept adult authority at work. Their youth society will always remain a positive part of the lives of these youngsters who spent a minimum of two years together and in the case of the Nachal soldiers, a maximum of five years. Such a chevra or peer group society which learns and works together was the key to the success of the rehabilitation program on a kibbutz.

The supportive nature of kibbutz living did aid the youth in adjusting to work and social activities, and the highly committed educational staff helped the group unit. In addition, the <u>madrich</u> guided the individuals in coping with and working out their problems. But all in all, it was the peer society which created the necessary change for a whole group of individuals who stayed together over a long period of time. The extended program and the follow-up support which was given by the Youth Aliyah Agency and the Tel Aviv Municipal Social Work Department also enabled the group to remain cohesive well after 1977. Almost all of the original twenty-one participants were in contact with one another at least until the latter part of 1980 when the research ended.

The fact that all the members envisaged joining the kibbutz after the conclusion of the program in 1977 and that most of them joined the <u>Nachal</u> as a <u>garin</u> is another major example of how the peer group succeeded in becoming a cohesive youth society wishing to settle permanently on the kibbutz that had nurtured it during the two-year program. All of these general truths, together with the statistical evidence presented in this chapter, reflect the concept of a peer group educational program which continued for an extended period of time in a highly supportive society and which succeeded in rehabilitating and socially integrating dependent and neglected Eastern Jewish youth in Israel.

THE RESULTS AND THEIR RELATIONSHIP TO THE PROPOSITIONS

Although there would be some difficulty in competing and eventually socially integrating with Western youth, the Ramat Hakovesh participants had taken strides forward in these areas. In comparison to the Barbour group members, their <u>madrich</u> Yitzchak, the teacher Hadas, and the social workers who knew them all felt that they had adjusted well to the Israeli Army, and their sights were well set on becoming future constructive citizens of the State.

It is necessary to repeat and to stress that the intent of my project was to trace the effect of a peer group approach on the attitudes of Eastern Israeli youth and to determine to what degree the youth who were in the kibbutz program of Youth Aliyah would become fully integrated and adjusted into Israeli society. Youth Aliyah's major goal has always been social integration, and in the 1970s its target population became Eastern Israeli youth from slum neighborhoods and welfare dependency families. To a certain extent, positive changes in attitudes toward social integration had occurred as a result of such a residential and long-range educational program. It also had become evident that the youth community which was developed during the two-year Youth Aliyah Program on Kibbutz Ramat Hakovesh created a highly committed group of youngsters motivated to serve the state in idealistic public tasks.

As I reviewed the goals of social integration theorists and their research on integration problems, it became evident that long-range residential and educational programs such as the Youth Aliyah could be effective in the long run in accomplishing the new task of the 1970s. During Youth Aliyah's history, the various forms of social rehabilitation had been changed to meet the new needs of the participants it served. With a theoretical background derived from other encampment programs' attempts to achieve social integration, I found that I was also able to apply new evaluational concepts to assess the attitudinal and behavioral changes in whole categories of individuals and systems. If the research can become the means by which the whole scientific community can influence the policy makers of social programs to initiate such programs as the Youth Aliyah Rehabilitation, it has achieved a major social role in the society of the 1990s.

As summarized in this chapter, the general effects on some attitudes and behavioral characteristics were such that the program goals of the social workers, teachers, and the madrich were reached. The social adjustment there was a successful completion of the program by a vast majority of the young

participants, and the majority served in the <u>Nachal</u> or successfully completed officer courses. The social adjustment and
public service goals of the program were also achieved because
the program's success can be viewed as the raising of a group of
former slum youth to the level of an elite ideological group
which could become socially well-integrated into Israeli society.
As Aaron Sharon pointed out, "There was not any doubt that
the accomplishments of the program certainly provided the
participants with an entrance into society as independent,
constructive, and even idealistic citizens who could socially
integrate into a highly competitive Western society, as in Israel
in the 1980s."

Without receiving every score of every questionnaire or
behavioral checklist, it is possible to follow the main lines of
change which did occur in attitudes and in behavioral patterns.
For instance, I did discover significant differences in the background realm between the Ramat Hakovesh and Barbour
groups and the Sderot middle class ethnically integrated <u>garin</u>.
Yet after two years, the professional strivings of the former
slum-dwelling youth of Jaffa and South Tel Aviv were much
greater than the other two groups. Their scores on the behavioral characteristics were as high as the Sderot group's in
general and low only in the same areas of "attitude toward
responsibility" and "status in social groups." Unlike the low
results (which were depicted in Behavioral Characteristic Lists)
in categories as "violence" and "unbridled sexual impulses"
among the Barbour group members and more often among the
Sderot group, the Ramat Hakovesh participants' scores were
generally higher in 1977. Even more significant was the overall
improvement in behavior from 1975 to 1977 and the behavioral
patterns during the army service of the Ramat Hakovesh group,
which demonstrated increased improvement in terms of social
adjustment.

I was also able to conclude that some changes had occurred
in the direction of social integration relative to the other two
groups, as I discovered many instances of attitude differences in
the areas of present social relationships to other groups and in
the area of long-range friendships and residence desires scored

highly by the Ramat Hakovesh group. There were also some positive differences on the responses which dealt with marrying people from other social classes and ethnic groups, which reinforced the above conclusion.

In general, the young participants from welfare dependent families, who in American terms would be considered "high-risk" youth, reached the same level as the Sderot group on questions dealing with idealistic commitment and social involvement in the State's needs. The former slum dwellers had scored far fewer points on background clusters than the equivalent number of participants of the same age and sex, but on a number of similar clusters in the attitudinal realms they scored as well as that different socioeconomic group on questions of ideological commitment and socially integrative attitudes.

The young participants of Ramat Hakovesh showed vast cultural and social upward mobility, which reached a level similar to that of youngsters who had finished high school and participated in a youth movement together, and were generally more socially integrated than other movement groups of its type. The Ramat Hakovesh garin then carried out the idealistic program of the Nachal, and in terms of the numbers who stayed in it until the end of that service, accomplished it to a greater extent than the Sderot group. These results led the people who worked with them from 1975 to 1980 to expect them to then enter into society as independent and concerned Israeli citizens.

The development of leadership potential in both the Sderot and the Ramat Hakovesh group was also mentioned in the previous sections, since the youth in both groups had learned in a strongly supportive and democratic environment, and many of them could develop later into positive leaders in our modern complex society. This added another dimension to the rehabilitation type of program. Such results or outcomes did not occur among the Barbour Street gang members, and their army records prove that in most cases there were problems in terms of their social adjustment. I also learned that a number of the Ramat Hakovesh youth who remained in the Nachal did so because of their feelings of belonging to a garin (the ultimate in peer group societies), and to a kibbutz; certainly some of them were also officer school caliber since they had received recom-mendations early in their army careers.

Having reviewed the results in an overall way, I was able to reach the specific conclusion that attitudes and the behavioral characteristics of the Jaffa-Tel Aviv slum youth, who came from welfare-dependent families of Eastern background, had been positively affected. The examples of this were in the realm of attitudes and approaches to the society in the present and in the future, as well as in the concrete area of behaviors which were changed over a long time period. It therefore became apparent to me that the social integration goals described earlier in this chapter were fulfilled by the Ramat Hakovesh group.

5
Federal Failures:
How Bureaucracy Hinders Progress

Children sleeping hungry while they shivered through their dreams
"Sing For Your Supper" by Doug Mishkin

In 1991 poverty and hunger stare one in the face throughout New York City's environs. One can also find them on the faces of other urban Americans. The number of poor people has risen in the United States for the first time in seven years (CNN Newsnight Report, September 26, 1991). The man I saw lying on the church steps and the garbage strewn all over the streets of New York City are symbolic of that condition.

It is not at all surprising then, that for every five children counted, one is poor and chronically hungry. Hunger and poverty cause many children to be chronically absent from school, create learning difficulties for them, and hinder their attempt to work when they drop out of school. Instead of meeting the standards of our President's New American Schools, they will commit 50 percent of such crimes as car theft and gang shootings.

These same young people do not participate in healthy recreational activities. They will instead play in the streets where crime and violence occur. Many youth often join street gangs since they have little family structure. They will grow up into serious criminals, beginning with petty delinquency, then crimes of violence which are associated with drugs, and finally graduate from the juvenile centers to the adult jails or straight into their early graves. In Boston, street crime prevention measures are now springing up, but the city officials admit to swimming against the tide in a society where violence is glorified and guns easy to acquire (ABC Evening News, August 31, 1991).

A good playground in San Francisco, and RBI (Runs Batted In), major league baseball's program which provides grass fields, uniforms, and coaches in Los Angeles, St. Louis and Harlem, are examples of oases in the "mean streets." Only a very few such excellent programs exist.

When the poverty-stricken children give birth to other children, many of them die in infancy, or become so physically ill that they are unable to work by the time they reach their teens. At the same time, libraries and recreational centers in New York and elsewhere are closing, but the police force remains the number one priority of our cities.

Is the United States regressing? Detroit is crime-ridden and has been getting worse. According to one savvy New York police officer, as Detroit goes in crime, so goes the rest of America seven years later. The question then becomes how can that vicious cycle be broken—the cycle of poverty and hunger, lack of educational opportunities, school failures, lack of work, and crime which continues to revolve around the hub of our urban centers?

Big Brother and Sister organizations with fine groups of mentors, the Police Athletic Leagues, major league baseball programs, and some unique nonprofit agencies can succeed in damming up the leaking walls for a short period of time, but these groups are usually low on funds and on highly qualified staff to follow-up on good programs. Often their successes are short-lived. Has the well-funded Job Training Partnership Act (J.T.P.A.) leadership provided enough monies or tried to recruit a large percentage of eligible teens from the major urban populations where they live? Some directors in the highest positions of such governmental bureaucracies do not even recognize that such "invisible" youth exist; therefore many potentially good programs have faced major federal and local cutbacks or lack of start-up monies in the 1980s. These facts have been common knowledge among those active in youth work in the United States. Politicians pay lip service to the problems of our troubled youth.

There has not been a change to rectify the nightmare of our children in chaos, and their numbers continue to multiply. How will it end?

Some concrete proposals and a support system of government, private business corporations and individuals, professional and volunteer workers, and the community people who live every day with the difficult issue of high-risk youth must contribute to the solutions. However, let us first examine the many governmental restraints on inner city programs. When social agencies do try to make a difference and propose model programs to representatives of federal and state bureaucracies, the governmental leadership creates restraints.

One initial generalization that applies to most creative programs which have the ability to get started is that there is an inconsistent commitment of government to them. This does undermine their stability. It is not infrequent for programs to open their doors to high-risk youth based on promises from sources which control government funding and then to learn suddenly that the monies have been reduced or eliminated. Even though the Federal Government guarantees state that their J.T.P.A. allocations will not be reduced more than 10 percent in any one year, that does not prevent S.D.A.s (Service Delivery Areas) from making radical shifts in funding at the local program level from one year to the next.

It is also true that political promises are most unreliable. For example, Pennsylvania Governor John Casey had promised that if a unique alternative program was successful in the demonstration phase, the state would expand it. The criteria for success of the western Pennsylvania program were clearly spelled out and Penn State was hired to evaluate the three demonstration sites. Eighteen months after the demonstration period ended, however, Penn State had still not released the evaluation results, and the Governor had not taken any action to resolve the situation. Therefore, one social agency and other demonstration sites had to piece together the funding to keep that program alive until the state would act.

In my own experience, such good social agencies have assembled excellent staffs but were unable to pay them or could only hope that they could afford to work for two or three months until funding began. As in the Pennsylvania case, there was not a guarantee that funding would continue regardless of the evaluation results.

One of the major problems for the social agencies with long-range programs in urban areas is that J.T.P.A. neither explains to youth about the range of occupations available to them, nor does it adequately inform them about the diversity of training options open to them. Consequently, youth are not encouraged to set any goals to participate in the types of programs that will help them. In one year, 1987–1988, a highly motivated recruiter for a nonprofit social agency rapidly recruited and assisted over 400 youth aged seventeen to twenty-one to enter J.T.P.A. training. After he had easily exceeded the contracted limit, he was told to slow down the pace of his recruitment efforts.

Just before the 1988–1989 fiscal year, his social agency was forced to lay him off because the government office decided not to recruit nearly as many youth in the relatively moderate-sized eastern American city. Then the number of youth who were entering training programs diminished to a trickle (approximately 150 that year), and J.T.P.A. officials who had to rationalize not recontracting a good recruiter tried to convince educational and social agencies that there just were not many high-risk youth in the "mean streets" of the community.

Sometimes a well-organized social agency does secure funds through a county department, but the criteria under that funding source will be different from the state's criteria. The State's criteria require participants to be "economically disadvantaged." The department of development does not require such economic lines (which is good, some analysts say, since it provides diversity in a fine alternative program), but the county insists that participants be residents of that county and not live in the city. The shifting of and conflicting requirements have kept the number of people in such a program to a minimum.

In general, youth are shocked when they are confronted with the demands of getting accepted into government programs. High-risk children who never had been taught how to fill out even a one-page application, must complete eligibility determination forms, evidence of draft status, documentation of income, and then complete a full battery of tests. All of this paperwork is bizarre to them, and there is not enough time to finish it.

One of the ways which alternative programs succeed is by setting up a supportive environment which combines a variety of methods to teach high-risk youth life skills and academic and vocational skills. These services are provided to meet the needs of at-risk teens, but the bureaucratic interpretations of regulations discourage the teens and prevent the program goals from being reached. Two examples illustrate the rigidity and lack of cooperation among funding sources.

Example 1: A well-known social agency had an O.J.T. (On-the-Job Training) program for youth who needed and were capable of learning from paid work experience. However, the agency needed some assistance in learning how to prepare resumes and how to teach their clients to present themselves to employers. The agency had to drop the O.J.T. program when J.T.P.A. refused to allow it to combine classroom training, resume assistance, other educational activities, and O.J.T. According to J.T.P.A., if someone was ready for O.J.T., that person didn't need classroom training.

Example 2: A training program in Pennsylvania designed to help youth become entrepreneurs was funded by a variety of sources, including the Department of Welfare, Food Stamps, J.T.P.A., Control Data Corp., the Appalachian Regional Commisssion (A.R.C.), and the United States Department of Labor Women's Bureau.

A key part of the program was that each participant would have an equity share in their enterprise (put some of their own money into their business). The amount was very small because these were poor kids. The balance of the funds for their business was to come from a revolving loan fund with money from the A.R.C. A social agency and the State of Pennsylvania had to convince the federal government to allow the participants to have capital assets. (They were all on welfare and therefore the rules would not permit them to have excess resources for investment.) The federal officials never did grant a waiver. The state finally had to grant its own waiver. <u>More attention was paid to the requirement of funding streams than to the delivery of services paid for by those sources.</u>

Eleven months into the twelve-month program, the participants had prepared their business plans and were ready to borrow from the revolving loan fund. At this point the Pennsylvania officials told the social agency that the state could not legally handle the A.R.C. loan funds as had been agreed at the outset of the program. They said the agency would have to deal directly with A.R.C. This was a terrible setback to the progress of the students and jeopardized the entire program.

Why did the state agree to handle the loan fund in the first place? Why did the officials wait until the money was needed before revealing that the arrangement was contrary to regulations? Why do governmental bureaucracies at all levels restrain good social agencies from developing and fulfilling the goals of excellent educational programs for at-risk youth? There are no answers which make sense to educators who do attempt to integrate at-risk youth into American society as good citizens.

Government restraints also include J.T.P.A. barriers to good in-school programming for high-risk youth. Excellent programs have been recently facing the inflexibility, lack of understanding of how the educational system works, and the burdensome documentation demands of state and federal governments. In one state, a program functioning in four counties (it was ten before funding was reduced) has been grappling with the anomaly that J.T.P.A. only deals with children's ages, not their grades. Therefore, many failing sixteen-year-olds who are in danger of dropping out cannot enter programs aimed at helping sophomores, since J.T.P.A. has stipulated that such programs rehabilitate only fourteen- to fifteen-year-olds who have become sophomores. Also, in-school youth might be better served by vocational training while they are fourteen or fifteen, but only sixteen-year-olds can receive this training, according to J.T.P.A.

regulations.

Another area where J.T.P.A. and our government is not realistic in terms of rehabilitating in-school at-risk youth is a lack of understanding about progress over a long period of time. For example, just keeping students in school is real progress. However, J.T.P.A. does say that they must advance one grade in math and reading, plus be in school 120 days for a social agency to get credit. The requirement means that if a child is making some progress, but moves out of the school district before 120 days of attendence, the agency has failed and must record a negative termination—even if that student subsequently enrolls in another school and does well.

In addition, the program activity and termination categories do not fit the real life circumstances of students and programs. In one dramatic case, a program was able to record as a positive outcome a youth who left the program because he was convicted of murder. That same year, this program had to record as a negative termination a youth who had made much progress in his personal life, relationships, attitude toward school, and general academics.

Another area where bureaucratic barriers hinder decent programs with their rehabilitation efforts is the enrollment and verification process.

Proving eligibility is a time-consuming, confusing, and frustrating process for program staff, students, and their parents. Often low-income parents who work often do not keep their pay stubs and thus cannot provide income data. Also, there is not a document to prove family size, so parents must fill out a family-size affidavit and have it notarized. Most parents will not make the effort to do this.

Programs have tried to overcome some of these obstacles by using documentation accumulated from other programs. For example, one program for in-school youth discovered that students in the school lunch program had income and family-size documentation in their administrative folders at school. School officials were willing to duplicate this documentation for the J.T.P.A. program, so the students could participate. However, J.T.P.A. would not allow the use of these documents.

In the arena of work experience, all of 200 hours must be taken by J.T.P.A.-enrolled youth during one six-month period. Once they have started work experience, the clock cannot be stopped. This prevents students from having work experience during both their junior and senior years. As one program's director soon discovered, a peer-tutoring program in which seniors were tutoring sophomores and juniors was hindered from continuing over an extended period because juniors were not allowed to reenter after the six-month period ended, even though they had not used all the 200 hours of work experience for which they were entitled to receive pay.

Finally, in the area of spending we see that when federal or state governments set formulas for expenditures for special target groups, they reduce local flexibility in responding to the actual need. For example: the proposed federal J.T.P.A. amendment to require 65 percent of Title IIA to be spent on adults and 35 percent on youths. Currently, at least 29 percent has to be spent on youth, but local areas can spend more if the need warrants.

Labor Department commissions have also stymied good creative socioeducational programs by requiring that competency skills be imposed on curricula developed by local educators and psychologists. These competency skills or job-related competencies include, for example, learning "resources" and "systems." These competencies as described by the Secretary of Labor's Commission on Achieving Necessary Skills aim to improve public school students' job skills and to ready them for the job market. However, a noted economic writer, Robert Samuelson, analyzed them as "gibberish" (Samuelson, July 11, 1991, A15). He outlined for us the mastering of the "systems" as:

1. Understands Systems—knows how social, organizational, and technological systems work and operates effectively with them;
2. Monitors and Corrects Performance—distinguishes trends, predicts impacts on system operations, diagnoses deviations in systems' performance,and corrects malfunctions;
3. Improves or Designs Systems—suggests modifications to existing systems

and develops new or alternative systems to improve performance.

Samuelson stated "It gets an A for mumbo-jumbo." Senator William Bock, the commission's chairman, had previously declared: "We have the worst school-to-work transition of any major country," but according to Samuelson, our schools (and in my opinion our dedicated social agencies) are failing not because they do not teach "systems." The competencies which J.T.P.A. and the Labor Department commissions had reported on and installed at various times as requirements were considered by Samuelson and other professionals as: "so vague as to be worthless."

With the job market so tight in 1991 that even good B.A. students had stopped searching for summer entry level industrial positions, it became obvious to many concerned citizens that the high-risk youth would have much less chance this year than in 1990.

In that type of economy, teaching "systems" to high school students and high-risk dropouts does not make much sense. As Samuelson responds, the answer is that we should teach two kinds of skills: "A solid foundation in reading, writing, mathematics, sciences and history and good work and study habits." We have also learned from the Carnegie Commission on Science, Technology and Government that American change agents need to agree wholeheartedly with the fact that better teacher training and good alternative educational programs in highly supportive environments can succeed in rehabilitating youth when the types of basic skills which Samuelson suggest are actually taught.

Using remedial teaching methods, Youth Aliyah Rehabilitation Programs in Kibbutz in Israel did have excellent academic results, as well as job-teaching skill outcomes that educational evaluators have rated highly. We can envisage a very positive outcome and can achieve those results by teaching practical job skills, good values, democratic peer group methods, and high interest and relevant subject matter to our high-risk youth.

We cannot teach "systems," sophisticated "competencies," and the differences between right and wrong to high-risk individuals who can barely read, do not have enough to eat, cannot earn money at part-time jobs, and cannot be counseled in a supportive environment over an extended period of time.

Scholars and practitioners have proven the above points time and again to the public's representatives and government bureaucrats. Now it is time for the people to demand creative programs and strong community support to slice through the negative tendencies of those who, due to fear of change or political self-interest, continue to restrain the attempts and movements toward change which will rehabilitate America's large numbers of high-risk youth.

6
Snapshots of Chaos:
Personal Portraits of Pittsburgh

The children I write about in this chapter were born in the late 1950s or early 1960s, when I was graduating from a highly rated high school in Pittsburgh. My school later won a national award in the 1980s because of its academic excellence and its well-integrated ethnic and racial make-up. During that period of my life, I had not yet developed many survival skills, nor was I socially capable of choosing the lifestyle I wished to live. However, I was able to win an academic scholarship, have my own room and telephone at home, eat decent meals, and, more importantly, receive emotional support from my parents. My peers were bright and socially conscious, prepared for college, and anticipating the good life after acquiring a degree. This is not the model which describes the young people with whom I worked in Israel and America in the years 1976–1989.

Those high-risk American and Israeli youth never had family support, physical security, or success in school. Nor did they have the opportunity to learn how to survive in our upper- or middle-class American society. As the decade of the 1980s came to a close, the young men and women of the Hill District of Pittsburgh had not found job security, nor had they completed a G.E.D. or post-G.E.D. learning program. They were either in jail, in substance abuse rehabilitation programs (St.

Francis Hospital in Pittsburgh was one of hundreds of such centers where the children of chaos found themselves), or hidden in a ghetto of poverty with poor health and potential death at the door.

The diaries and biographies that follow will verify the above; the results in Tables A.1–A.6 will analyze the true conditions of South Tel Aviv youth in the 1970s before and after the rehabilitation program at Ramat Hakovesh.

Observations and direct experiences with youth in the courts or in special programs for which they were registered by probation officers opened my eyes as much as did the statistical results from many behavioral checklists, attitudinal questionnaires, test results, and interview schedules. Before I decided to write about those children in chaos, I had read an article by Mick Hinton of the Washington bureau of The Daily Oklahoman. It began, "They are the kids nobody likes." It continued, "Because they have gotten into trouble with the law, most of them will spend Christmas in group homes. And they are not likely to get any presents" (December 19, 1990, 5).

The suicide rate of teenagers in the United States in the 1990 is higher than it was in the 1950s. Moreover, it crosses class lines to include all children from dysfunctional families. However, the "category" of disadvantaged children who are eligible for local, state, and federal programs represents the vast majority of all the children in chaos. These are the children whose lives will be detailed in the pages that follow.

In the late fall of 1983, I attended a meeting of J.T.P.A. administrators in Pittsburgh. Many of them were surprised that the Three Rivers Youth Alternative Educational Vocational Program had been so successful and that the at-risk youth who were hopeless six to twelve months before had achieved so much in such a short time.

At the A.E.V.P., our staff organized committees which enabled the high-risk youth to acquire responsibilities in "our community." A few months into the program, we had "Early Morning Community Group" discussions and homeroom time, where imparted positive values and good communication methods. Of the three committees (decoration, activities, and resource), the one which became actively interested in learning about post-secondary school and employment options was the resource committee.

Its active students were C. R., who did enter the University of Pittsburgh; F. F. and C. H., who attended Duff's Business Institute; and R. C., who became motivated enough to talk about owning his own business and worked for six months for a large cleaning corporation. Over a period of several months in 1983, these students invited speakers, examined brochures, and visited schools. Other students who participated in committee work deco-rated the building, organized sports activities, car washes, parties, and the monthly award luncheons. In the three or four months that they were active, these committees provided a new democratic style for youth who had never been asked to help nor to belong to any public school committee or organization.

In April I recorded notes on many of our students, thus beginning a diary which became the camera that photographed my students' lives throughout the remaining months of Cycle II of the A.E.V.P. (This program was divided into two cycles which overlapped. Each one was six months.)

On April 26 I wrote:

In my class, B. S. is drawing pictures and doing math. He had a lot of creative energy but does not know how to channel it. L. T. is sucking her thumb. L., who was a dropout in a previous program, is visiting us to see if he should join ours. He is talking mainly to L. T. M. R. is trying to finish a reading assignment. He is from the Hill District and looks very poor and ragged. C. R. studies hard. He wants to graduate this year with a high school diploma. B. G. sits in front of the class and stares into space. He is Pitt-bound, he claims.

K. T., who flunked out of a business school, needs help in English. She lacks confidence. Although it is rainy and dreary this afternoon, some of the students are motivated enough to study. C. R. continues to strive to finish his social studies lesson. Civil Laws and Criminal Justice are his textbooks. The aforementioned students, along with R. C., A. H. and W. G., were on job sites this morning, as were many others who are from our Cycle I group. All of them had passed their G.E.D. tests the first time.

In early May we began to look for unsubsidized jobs for eighteen of our students or register them for postsecondary schooling. This proved to be a difficult task in the summer of 1983, since the unemployment rate was sixteen percent in February and by July was still at thirteen percent. We already knew that two students had a good chance to attain decent jobs, and we felt that with patience and perseverance, all of the eighteen would either enter school or find full-time unsubsidized work.

On May 9 at 12:30 I recorded: "I saw J. D. on the corner near our building. This Cycle II student yelled to me that he would come to class soon—after he had some cocaine. Of course, he said this in front of two of his friends, and he did not arrive to class that afternoon." (He never completed the program. In September, he left after failing to hold even one of three unsubsidized jobs.)

On that day in May I role-played two males so K. T. would try to speak in front of a group. Although she was shy, this worked. She had a story to tell, which she shared with four girls during our 9:00 A.M. homeroom period. She related her life story of being abandoned by her mother at age seven and living with foster parents or in residential homes. There are chapters which are depressing throughout "her novel." On May 20 I added: "To teach these young high-risk youth, one must forget lesson plans. It's flexible and adaptive action that works when it comes to teaching them."

Another case in my journal concerned

One young lady, T., who lost her baby for six months in a court case, [and] was acting out this week; but by Friday she had opened her book and had begun to study. She offered to help staff members to get other students to read. On Thursday, we had reviewed colleges and made signs for our upcoming car wash and bake sale. With a little push, some students took leadership roles. On Friday, which was a difficult day for our students, twenty youths were involved in five areas of study—math, reading, computer work, typing, and G.E.D. review.

A few days later I wrote that

eight youths may go Wednesday to take their G.E.D. test. J. B. was one who was capable, but he was more interested in gambling and making money in the streets. Three Rivers Youth had a big luncheon on Friday. C. J. sang beautifully, and F. F. and S. M. attended as our program's representatives. Lieutenant Governor William Scranton was the guest speaker. F. F. talked to him. She was honest and straightforward as our students usually are.

On June 2, I recorded the following in my diary:

F. F. and M. R. have problems at home. I see that they are friends who are growing up and sharing a common problem. Some of our students have mischevious and/or destructive natures. We do not have middle-class expectations of them. M. T. took home a pile of <u>New York Times</u>. He was a young person who "hooked" us. We adults were charmed by him. He never made it, however, since his legal problems eventually overtook him, and he had to flee from the city. We did receive some rewards, such as when H. M., who could barely read in December, received a G.E.D. in June, L. T. passed her test with a "60" in reading, and R. B. also passed his test. Later that year, Act Together reported to us that our program had a very high percentage of students who passed the G.E.D. Test.

I also liked the way R. R. studied this week. Teasing these young people such as R. R. provided good "give-and-take," when they teased us back. There were, however, very sad times, as when M. lost her baby. She spoke hocus-pocus that day after the funeral. She was an abused child, and when she first entered the program, she would act out as soon as someone said anything to her. It was, therefore, necessary to explain to her and to the other students the kinds of behavior which would not be tolerated.

From June 6 and 7 I recorded the following:

It made our work feel worthwhile to place students into the Summer Program of Community College of Allegheny County and Connelley Skill Learning Center. Our emotions swing like a pendulum—frustrated when some failed to try, and satisfied when others succeeded. We had to teach our children slowly and hope they would later help themselves. When we lost faith, Marsha reminded us that we were working with "high-risk" youth!

W. S. is supposed to be picked up on June 20 and taken to register at Connelley Skill Learning Center, but he cannot explain to me how to get to his house. R. did not show up for the C.C.A.C. interview, since she feared that she would lose the newly found security of her Hill House job, where she was scheduled to work until the end of July. J. I. came late for his first two college interviews, but finally registered after the third one.

I was to drive D. K. to the Community College to register. He never meet me, neither the first time at his house, nor the second time at a downtown corner. Finally, I convinced him to meet me at our school building, and we drove to his 2:00 P.M. appointment. After we returned to the school, he finished the application forms and mailed them. However, he did not take the placement test, so I had to arrange for a second opportunity.

These were examples of the "Fear of Success Syndrome," and I could feel the frustration seeping through me as I experienced them with him.

W. S., R. S., and S. B. did make it to their Connelley Skilled Learning Center's appointments, registered, and entered the program. I continued to feel that as soon as some students saw the gates of possible achievement opening up and leading down a path to a positive future, they would become frightened and back away. A few continued to try.

R. C., however, was motivated enough to get a haircut on June 29 and on June 30 to go to two interviews. After his first successful interview, his spirits were high, and as we drove across town, he described his dream of owning a maintenance company. As we crossed Charles Street, he waved to the girls, smiled, and said, "Ivan, that haircut really helped, didn't it?" He was hired by a cleaning corporation after the interview of June 30 ($3.65 was his minimum wage salary, but he did get a raise after six months). At the same time, R. L. was accepted at Duff's, and that business school waived the fifty dollar entrance fee, since I had requested that N.E.E.D. (Negro Education Emergency Fund) cover it until he received his loan. They complied and later also agreed to help us with bus transportation to Cheyney.

There were other positive moments during this time period. T. W. was accepted by Median Health Center Career School, and W. G. and A. H. were accepted by Duff's. Then, B. S. passed the entrance test at Duff's and began his rocky career from June 1983 to January 1984. He was so happy that day that he took a bus to our school and helped me clean the living room. R. B. was also interviewed by a cleaning corporation on June 30 and began to work cleaning office buildings in downtown Pittsburgh.

As I learned again this month (recorded June 30),

It is a tough world in which we live. A senteen-year-old brought in pornographic cards which we confiscated. Her mother was a hooker and her father a dope addict. She had a good job-site, and once went on an interview, putting on acceptable clothes just before she entered the building. (This took place approximately half a block away from the building, while Diane, the job developer's aide, looked on aghast.) When she left, she took off the skirt which she had added to her shorts.

C. R. is doing very well at the Children's Museum, but C. J. was upset by an employer and quit. She eventually sat down and listened to Diane and me and agreed to talk to the supervisor about what was bothering her, but she never did. C. R. and C. J. were always making efforts, but three years later still were not doing so well. C. R. did work part-time at his original job-site for three years, but as far as I know, never did get a job as an accountant's assistant, which was his goal. C. J. never was employed regularly, although she had a few part-time jobs from 1983 to 1986. These students had too many problems to overcome while in a six-month program. In addition, they needed therapy and vocational counseling for at least eighteen months to two years.

In mid-June the job-developer, counselor, and I reported to Marsha the extreme cases of absences in our homerooms. The job-developer had five students with four to seven absences; the counselor had four students with five to ten absences; I had three students whose absences had forced me to interrupt their program, because they already had missed three to six days. Three students had to eventually be dropped from our J.T.P.A.-funded program due to an extreme number of absences. However, the total picture was still positive as 78 percent of the students finished Cycle I and 65 percent finished Cycle II.

On June 22 I recorded the following news:

C. H. and S. M. were plugging away, and A. S., who was preparing to attend Cheyney, began to discuss career possibilities. L. G. took S.A.T. tests two weekends ago and was studying computer science with Clyde (our computer teacher) on a regular basis. His job-site was assisting Clyde to help other students. Diane helped C. M. find a place to study nursing. I just learned that L. G. did get the job at C.C.A.C. in the computer science department for four days a week. S. M. was hired by Three Rivers Youth as a secretary. In June I took M. T. for breakfast, and J. B. tagged along. We discussed their potentials. Both were con-artists, but if they could have left the juvenile crime system, they would have developed into good constructive citizens. J. B. said that he would like to study economics and became a stockbroker. The big push for me was to get him to pass the G.E.D. test before the program ended. M. T. also had to pass his G.E.D. in July and take the A.C.T. so that he could register for Cheyney. However, he was soon committed to a juvenile detention center for a previous crime. Although we did have contact with him a few years later, we never were able to help him in a follow-up period of our program.

At the end of June, A. S. and R. C. visited with the counselor at his house until 10 P.M. and finally filled out registration forms. On the previous Tuesday, A. S. had traveled to Cheyney, and on Thursday, he had held up his brochure and yelled,

"See, I'm going after it." So, this street guy whom I had taken to the hospital to get plastic surgery on a wounded hand and who had talked to me about his goal to go to college and play football professionally, finally said he was taking the first step. Tim had organized his "odyssey" to Cheyney. I helped him find a part-time job in my neighborhood until school would begin. He was so thankful that he offered to help me move that July.

On Thursday D. K., C. S., and C. J. were hired by a construction company. C. J. was so excited that she repeated, "I got a job" a few hundred times that day. D. K. was accepted at C.C.A.C. T. W. was accepted at Duff's the day before classes started, and B. S. and R. L. also began their studies in fashion merchandising. Both of these two young men were doing well at this point.

We had some problems to solve at the work-sites of R. R., B. G., and J. B. Time schedules and discipline on the job are not the forte of many high-risk youth and, of course, that is why they are high-risk. M. W., L. T., K. T., and F. F. were trained well enough and had direction. They were finishing their applications for grants. So were L. G. and D. H. Twenty-one out of twenty-six students had been placed by July 15, 1983. This was our deadline for Cycle I students.

On July 25 I recorded the following paragraph:

> I was alone at Perry House on July 25 as Marsha was on vacation and other staff members were ill. Diane came in to help me with job development work. F. F. was registered in a commercial art course at Connelley. O. P. is in trouble with the police but still hopes to get into the Army if he can get out of the situation. A. S. was accepted into Cheyney but now needs financial assistance for registration, transportation, etc. T. W. has a good job at a library, and M. is working in a hospital. It was hot and humid Thursday, and C. G., was acting out, since her appointment at Pitt Medical School was cancelled due to the interviewer not being able to arrive that day. This occurred after she had arrived for the interview, which infuriated her. I learned that M. H. would not be hired full time at G.R.I.P. [a glass-recycling program] because he is slow in reading, although he basically worked well. This proves again that we need a lot of time with our students to get them ready for society. Not a

new idea to us. D. H. was accepted at C.C.A.C. after much commotion and his handling his own affairs inside the college bureaucracy. M. W., J. G., and K. T. are sending in forms to C.C.A.C. We are now trying to place Cycle II students.

On August 5–12 I added:

A. S. arrived, and we scrambled to raise $300, which was the amount he needed to go to Cheyney. We helped him fill out an application for N.E.E.D. A. S. said that he would acquire the linen and the clothes if we could help him with the rest of his financial needs. He had learned the lesson that he had to help himself whenever possible.

In August A. H., T. W., R. J., J. I., F. F., R. O., and B. S. were on our lists to get part-time jobs. Half of these students were ready to attend Duff's Business Institute, and the others would attend C.C.A.C. or other accredited career schools. Sixty percent were hired after August 17 by a number of franchises. Twelve students were interviewed, and six were hired in one week. C. M. was hired on August 15. C. J., R. L., T. W., R. J., and N. G. had been hired immediately after the August 25 interviews. R. J. received a twenty-hour-a-week job at a clothing store and went to C.C.A.C. at the same time. She was one of the few students to succeed within a period of one year. M. R. was promised a three-day-a-week job at a veterinary hospital. This was another success story in the making.

Also in August E. J., T. W., R. L., and R. J. were hired immediately after being interviewed at Chuck-E-Cheese. W. S., B. S., F. F., and W. G. presented themselves well at the interviews, and the manager put them on a list to be hired as needed. Bus transportation, bus fare, and distance create difficulties for poor high-risk youth who begin at minimum wage jobs, and a number of them lost positions for that reason.

A. S. failed at that interview, and he did not seem to be trying since his confidence level or some other problem was hindering his motivation to work. R. C. was doing well, and his "success story" led him to ask me if I would ever write about him in a book. He, A. H., and I once discussed the value of writing about our lives, and I told him I would love to write about him and others in our program. We convinced him to open up a savings account, and the bank manager told him that a twenty-five dollar minimum was a positive way to begin. After five minutes, he agreed and opened it. What a triumph! I told him how proud I was of him.

B. S. was depressed in this late August period, since he did not get a job at Chuck-E-Cheese. M. R. did not have a chance because he looked too shabby, but we would work hard with him to succeed, and by the end of September, he was hired for one good full-time job.

Between August 27 and September 3, I recorded more notes:

> C. R. went for a few more interviews. He had the potential but was not getting himself together. In October, I lost track of him but later learned that he lived near A. S., and neither had been working. T. W. continued to study for her G.E.D.. She is becoming positive about going to a college in January 1984. M. arrives reguarly and is doing well on a job-site. She is due to have a baby in January. This week A. K., another Three Rivers resident, registered for the next semester at C.C.A.C. She wants to be a nurse. M. R. did go to an interview at the veterinary hospital and was hired for three days a week. He was honest, well-mannered, and better dressed than the previous time, and demonstrated how much he loved animals.

Our society has recently been learning that the lack of prenatal care of young girls among the high-risk youth population has created a very high black infant mortality rate. In Pittsburgh, for example, it has reached 29.7 per thousand. Overall, there has been an increase of 500 percent in illegimate births to teenagers since 1950. Anyone who is aware of the problems of high-risk youth understands when doctors who research infant mortality state that high-risk young girls do not come in for check-ups early in their pregnancy, do not receive proper nourishment, and finally, do not feel good about themselves and their lack of status in society. As stated earlier, high-risk youth never have a positive image of themselves.

Although we felt frustrated by job-site losses, we knew there were some successes with C. R., J. G., K. T., C. G., M. R., L. G., and R. B. It appears that 60 percent will be good employees on regular jobs, and 80 to 90 percent of our students had passed their G.E.D. tests.

On September 21 I was still adding paragraphs to my diary:

A. S. is looking for a job but calls suddenly and claims he still wants to go to Cheyney. The students know that the program is ending and are trying to find something to do. G. D. took all five G.E.D. tests, and Tuesday he went to interview at the National Cleaning Corporation. M. R. also went to the interview and both boys were hired at $4.95 an hour. We have all the plans in place and are confident that most of our students will have jobs if they follow up the opportunities. The percentages of the Cycle I students who have jobs or are going to school is very high. The problem of the second cycle group is that only sixteen students of the original 28 twenty-eight can be placed. Many people in the social work field believe that if we can place thirty-five to sixty-one students, it signifies that we have done very well under the circumstances. Easily, there would be much more to do if only we had an additional four to six months to work with the students, even if most of that time was strictly follow-up support groups. As it turned out, I continued to help W. G., T. W., B. S., D. H., and R. C. solve their problems, some of which were with the law enforcement agencies.

On September 26 I recorded that we still were helping L. G. get a work study grant and B. S. and L. T. to get part-time job applications. It was a great occurrence when B. S. was readmitted to Duff's Business Institute. C. J. was now ready to start her third full-time job and this one was with an established corporation.

S. H., C. G., and K. T. also were hired by the National Cleaning Corporation, and C. R. was offered a job at a variety club and later would be asked to work part time at the Children's Museum which had been his work site. He does make a good impression, is energetic, and gregarious. He can do a better job than many middle-class students, since he has a great deal of motivation to work at this new museum. M. R., M., and M. W. are all doing very well, and others, such as G. D., continue to do their best since being notified that they would be hired full time by the National Cleaning Corporation and still had a chance to pass the G.E.D. M. learned that she was going to have twins and was ready to drink a double.

On September 30 we had an end-of-the-year party, and every student who attended had succeeded in one way or another. M. baked brownies and dropped them off before going to visit her family. C. G. and S. H. asked for plants and promised to care for them. K. T. was appreciated at work and received a twenty-dollar gift when she completed the program at her job-site. M. R., R. B., G. D., L. G., and S. M. also came, and R. C. joined us, looking serious and speaking of others not "messing around" at work, since it would ruin his reputation.

B. W. also showed up and Marsha felt we should give him a certificate for completing the program. This really moved our rough nineteen-year-old drop-in. On October 10, he arrived again, as it was the day we gave out the last checks. It was gratifying to know most of the students, including F. F., B. S., and C. H., were doing well in school. C. R. was interviewed for a second job in September, and she also was progressing in school. In summary, many students had made progress, more than our own supervisors, the C.E.T.A. staff, and even we ourselves had expected.

From February 1984 until 1986, I continued to add to my diary. In February 1984, B. W. was seeking a job and was lucky enough to find one at a Gulf station. B. S. was still searching for one. W. G. was studying at Duff's Business Institute, and A. H. completed the same program's second quarter. R. C., a major character in our never-ending saga, was in the process of appealing his termination by a large company which later allowed him to receive unemployment compensation. How these young people arrived at their crossroads is partially a function of their social histories.

I did intend to delve deeper into those histories, but unfortunately these indiviiduals did not arrive at a number of scheduled interviews in 1986 and 1987. One who has worked with such young people can understand that their high-risk natures account for their lack of dependability in keeping scheduled appointments. Ironically however, they did call me if they needed help, especially when they were in desperate situations. This is also a natural characteristic of high-risk youth.

Six months had passed since the program ended, but the youth continued to surface. In April 1984, I saw R. C. again. He was upset, but later, when I kept our luncheon appointment (I bought him a cheeseburger and a coke), he was feeling better and hoping to be interviewed soon. He also expressed an interest in being the "peer counselor" in the new A.E.V.P. program, but not in learning the academic material. I countered by saying that participants have to go to both vocational and job skills classes. He had come over to my office at the Youth Center on March 22 and recounted to me some of his past experiences, after discussing his major problems and his feelings of being depressed, F. F., I learned, had left Duff's for personal reasons in late February. The elusive B. S. called me long distance on March 26. He was in New York washing dishes at a steak house. Apparently, he had left for that city some time in March. Later, he returned to Pittsburgh, as he said he would. He then joined the Job Corps in which he stayed until September. I could not locate F. F. at all, even when Duff's tried to help me. I felt that she was also becoming lost and facing a troubled future. Later, I found out how wrong I had been. She was employed and doing well.

R. C. called back in June and spoke to us twice. He also visited us twice, including once on his birthday when Marsha and I took him to lunch. He was not sure what he wanted to do, but he did agree to let Debbie, our job developer, work with him. He filled out job applications and promised to return. When he came back a second time with his friend A. S., a new A.E.V.P. program had already started. They helped us move a desk. Of course, I had to give them a dollar for three hot dogs, as they still were "survivors." I received a call later from A. S. asking for help in finding him a job. He was still a little belligerent, which was not unusual. He told me that he would go to Eat 'n Park Restaurant if I called the manager and put in a good word—which I did later in the week. R. C. and A. S. spoke to me about joining the Army Reserves. They were getting desperate. It appeared as if they were running out of choices. R. C. left his address and requested that Debbie write to him. I told him to come in again, and we would talk even though I felt that he was being negatively influenced in the streets and would remain out there. As of July 6, I had not heard from him again. The unemployment rate had dropped, and many more young people were working during the hot summer, but R. C. was facing his own chaos. He was collecting unemployment from the state.

The only good news which I heard in June was that despite the fact that L. G. failed a few subjects, he was hired as a regular employee of the computer service department of C.C.A.C. He was doing well there, according to the counselor, Leonard Allen, who tried to call it "our success" when I said it was one of his successes! At least we did have a few achievements six months after the program had ended. I would have hoped that by June 1984 there would have been more.

Later in the fall of 1984, we heard occasionally from R. C. and B. W. Both were out of work by the winter, but B. W. was still living with his girlfriend and actively looking hard for work. C. R. was working one day a week at the Children's Museum and looking for a job as an accountant, bookkeeper, or secretary. He had finally received a diploma, and his enthusiasm was expressed by his search for work and by his obvious desire to better himself. He continued to call me in the winter of 1984-1985. He was still working at the Children's Museum.

I also want to mention that C. H. had finished her studies and had a certificate. A male friend of hers called me at home to demonstrate a cleaning tool for sofas and rugs, and she spoke to me first. She sounded good and fulfilled with plans to return to her native Alabama. L. T. was working in 1986 at a southside restaurant, but R. C. was still unemployed in that year, and the cycle of poverty engulfed him. The last few times I spoke to him, he was depressed. In 1986, I realized that I had not seen B. W. for a year. My impression was that he was on the streets, which is to say that he was not rehabilitated at all. M. W., who had been friendly with L. T., also said she would be interviewed, but she never appeared. She also never finished C.C.A.C., although she did complete a job search program at J.T.P.A. She told me that she never was ready for college in the first place.

In general, the majority of our students were just surviving, but many were still in the ranks of the poor, possibly to be stuck there until they died. This ending is the true picture of the results of good educational programs which, however, are not granted the necessary funding for professional follow-up. Nor is it realistic to expect such support in the future. The statistical success realized and the hope for the future that the staff had for the students were not enough to ensure that they would overcome their disadvantages and past failures.

If some of the students could manage to escape from the unemployment-depression-poverty cycle, as C. H. appeared to be doing, they then would be the exceptional cases—people whom we helped, but whose skills, abilities, and determination overcame society's failure to deal justly and thoroughly with their problems. L. G. is another example of successful completion of studies and a job, thanks to the positive professional help he received at C.C.A.C. In my view, however, the final total picture is not a positive one; and the emphasis of society must shift rapidly in order to save our young invisible heroes and heroines before we lose another generation. One only has to read the national statistics released in 1990–1991 to verify the fact that we are still far from breaking the cycle of crime, poverty, failure, and an early death of America's youth.

I did not record in my diary any more news about my students of 1982–1983 until 1987. Finally, some news began to reach me through networks I had established without realizing it. In the summer of 1987, C. H. called to ask my help in retrieving her G.E.D. diploma from her father so that she could enter the army. Her father had not allowed her to stay with him in Alabama, so she had to return to Pittsburgh. When she was seventeen and pregnant, she had dropped out of school and now at age twenty-one, she hoped her aunt would take care of her four-year-old son. From Duff's Business Institute, she had received a health care specialist certificate, and her plan in the summer of 1987 was to study to be a medical assistant in the U.S. Army. However, because her father refused to surrender her G.E.D. diploma, and the Harrisburg Office of Education could not give her another one, her plans were not realized. She did find work as a resident care technician at a child development center in Pittsburgh, and her plans were to go back to school to study nursing.

C. H. also told me that C. M. was now a nurse's aide but had recently lost a child. C. M. had graduated from the Western Pennsylvania Health School and was working in the health field. She was supporting two children by herself. R. B., the father of C. H.'s child, was unemployed. R. C. was washing dishes at a restaurant in Oakland and still living at home.

B. S. had called me a few months earlier from St. Francis Hospital to which he admitted himself for drug addiction. Previously, I had learned that he had been working at a supermarket, and, typically, he called me once to borrow ten dollars.

K. T. was now married and had one child, as was J. T. whom I did see working as a messenger in downtown Pittsburgh. A. S. was a disc jockey on weekends, but did not have a steady job. C. R. had a child and was working. C. H. said that he was trying to get custody of the child from his ex-girlfriend. B. W. had a wife and a child, and at times worked as a painter.

The news that R. C. was a policeman was mind-boggling and remains, to this moment, unverified.

The A. H.'s and R. C.'s could be fine citizens of our land, but they are, by far, the small minority; for the cycle of poverty, crime, and despair was still the main theme in the 1980s.

We need, as a total society, to break that cycle before it penetrates our complacent cocoon. If and when it does, I am now certain that America will be overwhelmed. The signs of such a tragedy were with us in December 1988, and in September 1991, were more ominous.

In 1990–1991, I had my own personal experience mentoring an eighth grade boy from an alternative middle school. This young person also needed counseling and a friend, but mainly had to be in a supportive environment. As I am writing this paragraph, he is doing well in a regular school program and is attempting to keep his grades up and play on a basketball team. His family has dysfunctional elements, and there are no assurances that he will be a constructive citizen who will not end up in the juvenile justice system. I had spent one day a week counseling him, shooting baskets with him, and just being a friend. In my mind, however, follow-up work with him and hundreds of thousands of other youth like him must occur in a strongly supportive community environment with professional care, if we wish to continue to make progress in rehabilitating our children in chaos.

7
Conclusion

The long-range residential educational programs using peer group approaches within highly supportive environments definitely created needed changes. These programs are able to rehabilitate youth from disadvantaged and welfare-dependent families. To adjust and socially integrate within the Israeli society was the goal of one such program. This goal, in addition to others and multiplied by many similar programs could close the social gap which is continually widening in a society that feels more than ever the negative manifestations of the gap's constant growth. From the vantage point of one who has seen similar programs on both sides of the ocean, it appears that the time has come to initiate more than the four or five programs a year in <u>kibbutzim,</u> as well as the few special ones in New Jersey or western Pennsylvania.

There is no doubt that educational changes lead to social changes and will create social integration as the social gap is closed. Young people reared in the residences of Youth Aliyah have always comprised the more problematic element in their age group. Other contingents in Israel and abroad usually consist of young people who grew up under normal circumstances. Therefore, Youth Aliyah prepared for the future a community of children and young people living under exceptional and problematic circumstances. The children were the refugees, the displaced, the homeless, or hopeless, as the "high-

risk" youth in America are today. In the 1970s, they were referred to as children who came from culturally backward families, or from socially and emotionally unstable homes. The
programs at Highfields, New Jersey, or in Pittsburgh, Pennsylvania, constitute "ungraded schools" as Youth Aliyah comprised
in the 1970s the "ungraded school" of the community and the
land of Israel. The follow-ups of the graduates of programs
similar to the Rehabilitation Program at Ramat Hakovesh show
that unlike routine employment for graduates of regular training programs for youth abroad, Youth Aliyah did not consider
the average outcomes only as success.

Routine employment became the minimum, and among the
graduates, no lower that 5 percent became college professors.
The feeling in the case of Youth Aliyah's policymakers is that
the conditions of hardship, oppression, and suffering never im-
paired a young person's capacity to grow, to adapt, and to be
trained; the staffs have never regarded their work as an ordi-
nary job where clocks are punched in return for a paycheck.
The other ingredients for success in the Kibbutz and other
similar programs were that they were open to new ideas and the
need for constant change. They acknowledged errors made and
learned the relevant lessons early in the program's development. The type of commitment and professional flexibility and
accountability are rare ingredients in agencies such as Youth
Aliyah; therefore their ability to succeed in closing the social
gap in western democratic societies is reasonably assured, if
policymakers and funding agencies continue to support the
staffs of such specific programs.

Neither in America nor in Israel do we wish to see the gaps
widen and the vulnerable and helpless youth remain without the
ability to help themselves and to become constructive, concerned, and contributing citizens. Knowing the type of socioeducational programs that can create change, we need to
implement them soon and wherever it is possible.

We also realize that there are styles of work and educational
approaches which programs in the United States and Israel
both use successfully. There is no question that committed
staffs and positive methods of the educational and social work

fields also exist on both sides of the ocean. Only by expanding social programs of the type this book has described can we hope to help the young save themselves. The people who control funding and the communities who can support such programs must begin to lend their hands and hearts, if there is to be a major contribution in this decade to an essential human field.

Appendix I
Agencies Receiving
"Act Together" Grants

Source: "Act Together," a Nonprofit Organization in Washington

ALABAMA DEPARTMENT OF YOUTH SERVICES, MT. MEIGS, ALABAMA

The state government was ready for block grants, and the new federalism was demonstrated in Alabama as the use of public funds was maximized for high-risk youth services.

The Alabama Department of Youth Services' (D.Y.S.) "Prime Time" project was a statewide effort in which D.Y.S., the state C.E.T.A. office (J.T.P.A. became the Labor Department's new name for C.E.T.A. in the 1980s), the state Mental Health Department, and the State Department of Conservation worked together to provide a treatment program for incarcerated youth.

Prime Time features long-term, structured services that are realistic alternatives to institutionalization. The services include a wilderness course, group home placement, parent training, and community reintegration.

The individual youths in the project are carefully screened and assessed. After being placed in small groups, they move through the program as a unit, thereby avoiding the continuous and disruptive readjustments that youth traditionally experience in moving from placement to placement.

Family involvement and area work experience in conservation as a part of vocational training are other unique Prime Time components which serve to improve each young person's chances for successful reentry into the community.

BRIDGE OVER TROUBLED WATERS, INC., BOSTON, MASSACHUSETTS

Points of entry, varied and numerous, are made available to 3,000 high-risk youth annually by Bridge's multiservice program, in operation since 1970. Specifically, each service that Bridge offers functions as an entry point to additional services. One way Bridge connects with high-risk youth is to take medical services and drug and alcohol counseling to the "combat zone" and street hangouts where high-risk youth gather.

The client-flow pattern that Bridge uses enables high-risk youth, who generally require a variety of services, to present to the program their most pressing problems—housing, food, education, employment. Once the youth are in the program, Bridge can respond to their needs holistically.

Bridge's many services are provided by a committed, cohesive staff. The agency credits it well-organized staff development and training program with producing a staff who work together in delivering services and who share resources in a professional and efficient way.

Volunteers play a major role in providing services. Recruited primarily through word of mouth, and also through extensive media and public support, volunteers have a clear sense of the agency's goals and mission, of their role in delivering services, and of how important they are to the success of the program, both as service providers and as advocates.

THE CONNECTION, MINNEAPOLIS, MINNESOTA

A university and a public high school partnership is "the connection" to making education work for high-risk youth. The

Connection began in 1978 as an expression of the University of Minneapolis's commitment to serve youth with learning problems.

The Connection clearly demonstrates that when community agencies and institutions work together, results are produced. For example, linking with the local chamber of commerce led to the joint hiring of a job developer; with the board of education, the information of an accredited course relevant to high-risk youth; and with a C.E.T.A. prime sponsor, to the development of a preemployment classroom experience. Thus, youth in the program received the kinds of services that help them stay in school or get a job.

Completing the connection are the concerned college students who serve as case managers to youth in the program. Training and assistance given by a paraprofessional supervisor enable these college students to track and support the youth through the Connection, while providing the college students with a unique and credited placement as they prepare for their careers.

DIVISION OF CHILDREN'S SERVICES, LEXINGTON, KENTUCKY

As a public agency that went beyond its statutory mandates to serve troubled youth, the Division of Children's Services (D.C.S.) formed a unique, responsive, and reciprocal partnership with the communities it serves. D.C.S. earned its place in the Act Together demonstration through its innovative direct-service strategies and management improvement.

In D.C.S.'s new Juvenile Resource Center, for example, high-risk youth and potential employers met and learned about each other. Other center activities included preemployment assessment, counseling, and training, as well as employment training.

Working closely with and keeping the lines of communication open with private and other public agencies was another D.C.S. priority. By convening a Youth Service Consortium of public and private agencies, D.C.S. created a system for generating the interagency awareness neceassary to reduce duplication of ser-vices and red tape. Internally, D.C.S. developed new management initiatives, and established a computerized management information system which provided current data on youth and youth services.

From putting its "Career Passport" system into operation–a system that works in supporting youth as they enter the job world–to leveraging community support (e.g., church groups and the United Way), D.C.S. provided the kinds of services which realistically addressed and met the needs of Lexington's high-risk youth.

NEW LIFE YOUTH SERVICES, CINCINNATI, OHIO

Community support and involvement in programs that serve delinquent youth are major focuses of New Life Services. Through New Life, adjudicated youth and youth with multiple problems receive training, meaningful job skills, and other services that contribute to self-sufficiency and self-confidence. The youth, in turn, contribute to their community through a unique employment and training program called the Freedom Factory.

In the Therapeutic Products Division of the Freedom Factory, youth produce therapeutic aids which they are often able to observe in use. The young people thus not only develop marketable skills, but they are able to see at first hand how their work contributes to the quality of people's lives. Seeing the good they do and receiving public praise in United Way film clips give the youth a special experience–that of knowing they make a difference with people and that they have a place in the community.

Corporate and community support has been a keystone in establishing the Freedom Factory's Industrial Products Division, a self-supporting enterprise which manufactures industrial pallets for businesses in greater Cincinnati. Corporate contributions were fundamental in helping New Life to purchase the plant facility. A community economic development organization is also a financial partner in the operation.

THE SHELTER, SEATTLE, WASHINGTON

That street youth and runaways are characteristically "antisystem" does not deter the Shelter from reaching out to this difficult population. The Shelter focuses on outreach to youth on the streets and on providing short-term shelter services, including intensive individual and family counseling.

To provide a full spectrum of services to street youth, runaways, juvenile prostitutes, and other high-risk youth, the Shelter links up with other community agencies that provide such services as employment placement, drug and alcohol counseling, alternative education, additional short-term residential services, and early intervention in the schools.

Linkages, based on a referral system that uses an interagency financial match system, bring together various providers as they are needed. Specifically, the other agencies in the referral provide services to the Shelter's youth at only 50 percent of the cost that the agency ordinarily incurs.

The linkage approach eliminates costly program development time, avoids duplication of services, allows available funds to be used for direct service provision, and, most important at all, enables the youth to receive high-quality care in all areas.

The Shelter's success in meeting the service needs of its target population is strengthened by the organization's ability to work with other agencies and organizations which are not part of its direct service system. These include churches (the Coalition on Youth in Crisis), volunteer groups (the Association of Voluntary Executives), and key policymakers (the Seattle Mayor's Office and the state Department of Social and Health Services).

Ultimately, through education and job placement, through being reunited with their families and through other positive outcomes, the high-risk youth whom the Shelter serves can turn to rewarding and productive lifestyles and activities.

Appendix II
An Operational Definition
of Public Service

In defining public service, one has to arrange a scale which can be concretely applied to public service under various possible conditions in many different lands. For example, in Israel, where this study was carried out, young people (high-school age) do voluntary patrol service in urban and rural areas alike. (Some of the youth of the street group from which one of the samples was taken also occasionally did such service in the South Tel Aviv area, and it carried a high prestige value for them.) Most Israelis have been educated toward the values of volunteerism and public duty for the nonformal means of extra-curricular school activities, paramilitary and scouting organizational programs of the gadna (paramilitary youth training group) or Tzofim (scouts), or informally by public service announcements such as those on joining Mishmar Ezrachit (civilian guard). In other countries, however, more self-interest is evident, and there has been a lessening of public service activities since World War II. Only a minority in some of the advanced Western countries or in some Third World countries which have been independent for many years are interested in giving a high priority to public service. Therefore, a realistic definition of the term "public service" must be concrete enough to fit the various patterns, which include highly dedicated minorities in the more established countries as well as higher percentages of volunteering citizens in countries like Israel, which still maintains a high level of pioneering values and a high degree of carrying out the social ideals of the society.

Appendix III
Behavioral Checklist for
Social Integration Attitudes

1. The subject often engages in discussions with people of different ethnic origin than his own.

   ( )YES ( )NO

2. The subject often expresses distrust of people of other ethnic groups.

   ( )YES ( )NO

3. The subject openly favors an integrated urban neighborhood where he will live.

   ( )YES ( )NO

4. The subject expresses opposition to the use of political demonstrations to gain ethnic rights.

   ( )YES ( )NO

5. The subject is socially involved with people of his/her age who belong to ethnic groups other than his own.

   ( )YES ( )NO

6. The subject advocates marrying within one's own ethnic group.

   ( )YES ( )NO

7. The subject often participates in social activities with people of different socioeconomic classes.

( )YES ( )NO

8. The subject advocates marriage outside one's own socio-economic class group.

( )YES ( )NO

9. The subject participates in many leisure time activities which are not usually considered those of his/her own socio-economic class.

( )YES ( )NO

10. The subject, in your opinion, will be a good citizen of Israel after he/she finishes the period of his/her army services.

( )YES ( )NO

Appendix IV
Public Service Commitment
Questionnaire B

A sample of six of the questions of the Public Service Commitment Questionnaire (Part B) are listed below. They are representative of the nineteen questions of the questionnaire.

1. How do you accept the fact that you are a member of the Jewish people?
   (a) With pride. It is a privilege to be a member of the Jewish people.
   (b) It's an existing fact.
   (c) So it is my fate and it's my task to make the best of it.
   (d) This is a negative point.
   (e) I hope to find a way to free myself from it in the future.

2. In your opinion, how important is it for a Jew who lives in Israel and wants to be called a Zionist, to do each of the following actions? Circle the appropriate letter.
   > VI–Very Important
   > I–Important
   > NV–Not Very Important
   > NI–Not At All Important

VI I NV NI (a) Serve in the army
VI I NV NI (b) Help absorption of new immigrants
VI I NV NI (c) Help to diminish the social gap
VI I NV NI (d) To feel identification with the State

VI I NV NI (e) To love the State of Israel
VI I NV NI (f) To fight negative phenomena in the State
VI I NV NI (g) To leave Israel to convince Jews outside the
State to immigrate to Israel
VI I NV NI (h) To try to understand the conditions under
which Jewry lives
VI I NV NI (i) To help in the development towns in Israel
VI I NV NI (j) To feel belongingness to the State of Israel
VI I NV NI (k) To help collect money for the State outside of
Israel

Of all the actions above, which one seems most important?

3. Do you think after you finish your army service that you will
be active in political or public life?
   (a) Positively yes
   (b) I would like to be active
   (c) I do not think I will be active
   (d) Positively no

4. Do you feel that Israel is a democratic state?
   (a) Definitely yes
   (b) Yes, but not in every sense of the word
   (c) Not so much
   (d) Definitely not

5. Many people speak about their desire to live permanently
outside the State of Israel. Would you also wish to do so?
   (a) I very much want to live outside of Israel permanently.
   (b) I would somewhat desire to live outside of Israel permanently.
   (c) I would not very much desire to live outside of Israel
permanently.
   (d) I would definitely not desire to live outside of Israel.

6. In your opinion, do you think it is necessary to encourage marriages between the different ethnic groups in Israel?
   (a) Definitely yes
   (b) Yes
   (c) No
   (d) Definitely no

TABLE A.1

Spearman Brown Split Half Test Results

Odd-Numbered Questions		Even-Numbered Questions		
Totals	Rank	Totals	Rank	D
35	1	34	1	0
32	2	34	1	2
31	3	33	3	0
31	3	31	4	1
31	3	31	4	1
30	6	29	6	0
29	7	28	7	0
29	7	28	7	0
29	7	28	7	0
28	10	26	10	0
28	10	26	10	0
28	10	25	12	2
27	13	25	12	1
26	14	25	12	2
25	15	25	12	3
25	15	24	16	1
25	15	24	16	1
20	18	23	18	0
20	18	23	18	0
20	18	20	19	1
20	18	19	20	2

$D^2 = 256$ $R = .98$ $p < .01$

TABLE A.2

Results of Israeli Army Intelligence Tests for Ramat Hakovesh Graduates

Name	School Grade Level	Level of Hebrew	G I Test Score*	Army Rank	Army Job	Times AWOL	Days AWOL
L.A.	10	9	62	Private	Clerical	-	-
Y.P.	7	7	40	Private	Administrative Worker	-	-
Y.D.	8	7	51	Private	Front Line Soldier	-	-
M.C.	7	7	51	Corporal	Administrative Worker	-	-
M.C.2	10	8	62	Private	Front Line Soldier	-	-
D.L.	10	8	70	Private	Stock Boy in Warehouse	1	23
E.M.	9	8	52	Corporal	Administrative Worker	-	-
N.Y.	10	8	52	Private	Clerical	-	-
R.A.	7	5	20	Corporal	Civil Defense	-	-
A.N.	8	8	40	Corporal	Commander of Small Unit	-	-
A.Tz.	10	9	51	Private	Civil Defense	-	-
R.A.	8	9	62	Sergeant	Commander of Small Unit	-	-
Y.S.	10	7	61	Sergeant	Commander of Small Unit	-	-

* Indicates score on Israeli Army Intelligence Test

Times illegally off the base for these thirteen soldiers was 17 during their entire army service for an average of just over 1 time per soldier.

Source: Israeli Army

TABLE A.3

Results on Social Integration Based on Responses to Questionnaire A (June-July, 1977)

Section	Ramat Barbour Hakovesh Total Avg.		Sderot Total Average		Total Average

I   Questions dealing with positivity of attitudes and relationships to social and ethnic groups other than own group.
(Average Responses to Questions 13,14,15,20, 21,22,23,27)

	Ramat Barbour Hakovesh		Sderot		Total
13 ----- 5		13 ----- 4.0		13 ----- 4.8	
14 ----- 5		14 ----- 4.5		14 ----- 5.0	
15 ----- 3.3		15 ----- 3.3		15 ----- 3.1	
20 ----- 3.6	3.9	20 ----- 4.1	3.8	20 ----- 3.1	3.9
21 ----- 4.1		21 ----- 4.0		21 ----- 4.4	
22 ----- 3.7		22 ----- 3.7		22 ----- 4.4	
23 ----- 3.6		23 ----- 3.5		23 ----- 3.8	
27 ----- 2.5		27 ----- 2.7		27 ----- 4.2	

Section	Ramat Barbour Hakovesh Total Avg.		Sderot Total Average		Total Average

II   Questions dealing with positivity of attitudes on long-range questions -- place of residence and friends.
(Average Responses to Questions 16,17,26)

16 ----- 3.5		16 ----- 3.4		16 ----- 2.4	
17 ----- 3.5	3.2	17 ----- 1.6	2.1	17 ----- 2.8	2.8
26 ----- 2.5		26 ----- 1.3		26 ----- 3.2	

III   Questions dealing with positivity of attitudes toward social integration in regard to personal life situations.
(Average Responses to Questions 18,19,24,25)

18 ----- 3.7		18 ----- 3.7		18 ----- 2.5	
19 ----- 4.8	3.8	19 ----- 4.2	2.1	19 ----- 2.5	4.0
24 ----- 3.3		24 ----- 3.2		24 ----- 3.5	
25 ----- 3.4		25 ----- 2.7		25 ----- 5.0	

Results on Upward Social Mobility Based on Leisure Time Responses

The scores of the nine Ramat Hakovesh participants were:
50, 60, 64, 67, 75, 75, 80, and 80. The average was 70.

The scores of the seven Sderot participants were:
66, 75, 79, 80, 83, 89, and 91. The average was 80.

Chi Square Test results of Leisure Time answers:

	Ramat Hakovesh	Sderot	Total
Above 74 Average	$5 - \dfrac{\left(\dfrac{(9 \times 11)}{16}\right)^2}{\dfrac{9 \times 11}{16}}$	$6 - \dfrac{\left(\dfrac{(7 \times 11)}{16}\right)^2}{\dfrac{7 \times 11}{16}}$	= 11
Below 74 Average	$4 - \dfrac{\left(\dfrac{(9 \times 5)}{16}\right)^2}{\dfrac{9 \times 5}{16}}$	$1 - \dfrac{\left(\dfrac{(7 \times 5)}{16}\right)^2}{\dfrac{7 \times 5}{16}}$	= 5
N	9	7	= 16
	Chi Square Result: 1.42	$p < .30 - .20$	

TABLE A.5

Results of the Three Groups' Responses Relating to Background, Public Service Commitment, Ideology, and Social Adjustment

A. Background

	Ramat Hakovesh	Sderot	Barbour	Total
Above 2.37 Average	$2 - \left(\dfrac{(9 \times 10)^2}{(23)} \right)$ $\dfrac{9 \times 10}{23}$	$7 - \left(\dfrac{(7 \times 10)^2}{(23)} \right)$ $\dfrac{7 \times 10}{23}$	$1 - \left(\dfrac{(7 \times 10)^2}{(23)} \right)$ $\dfrac{7 \times 10}{23}$	$= 10$
Below 2.37 Average	$7 - \left(\dfrac{(9 \times 13)^2}{(23)} \right)$ $\dfrac{9 \times 13}{23}$	$0 - \left(\dfrac{(7 \times 13)^2}{(23)} \right)$ $\dfrac{7 \times 13}{23}$	$6 - \left(\dfrac{(7 \times 13)^2}{(23)} \right)$ $\dfrac{7 \times 13}{23}$	$= 13$
N	9	7	7	$= 23$

Chi Square Result: 9.47 $p < .01$

B. Professional Strivings

	Ramat Hakovesh	Sderot	Barbour	Total
Above 1.5 Average	$9 - \dfrac{\left(\dfrac{9 \times 11}{23}\right)^2}{\dfrac{9 \times 11}{23}}$	$2 - \dfrac{\left(\dfrac{7 \times 11}{23}\right)^2}{\dfrac{7 \times 11}{23}}$	$0 - \dfrac{\left(\dfrac{7 \times 11}{23}\right)^2}{\dfrac{7 \times 11}{23}}$	= 11
Below 1.5 Average	$0 - \dfrac{\left(\dfrac{9 \times 12}{23}\right)^2}{\dfrac{9 \times 12}{23}}$	$5 - \dfrac{\left(\dfrac{7 \times 12}{23}\right)^2}{\dfrac{7 \times 12}{23}}$	$7 - \dfrac{\left(\dfrac{7 \times 12}{23}\right)^2}{\dfrac{7 \times 12}{23}}$	= 12
N	9	7	7	= 23

Chi Square Result: 16.6 $p < .001$

C. Ideological Scale

	Ramat Hakovesh	Sderot	Barbour	Total
Above 1.5 Average	$4 - \dfrac{\left(\dfrac{9 \times 11}{23}\right)^2}{\dfrac{9 \times 11}{23}}$	$4 - \dfrac{\left(\dfrac{9 \times 11}{23}\right)^2}{\dfrac{9 \times 11}{23}}$	$4 - \dfrac{\left(\dfrac{9 \times 11}{23}\right)^2}{\dfrac{9 \times 11}{23}}$	= 12
Below 1.5 Average	$5 - \dfrac{\left(\dfrac{9 \times 12}{23}\right)^2}{\dfrac{9 \times 12}{23}}$	$3 - \dfrac{\left(\dfrac{7 \times 12}{23}\right)^2}{\dfrac{7 \times 12}{23}}$	$3 - \dfrac{\left(\dfrac{7 \times 12}{23}\right)^2}{\dfrac{7 \times 12}{23}}$	= 11
N	9	7	7	= 23

Chi Square Result: 0.41

D. Social Scale

	Ramat Hakovesh	Sderot	Barbour	Total
Above 1.4 Average	$4 - \dfrac{(9 \times 12)^2}{(23)}$ $\dfrac{9 \times 12}{23}$	$3 - \dfrac{(7 \times 12)^2}{(23)}$ $\dfrac{7 \times 12}{23}$	$5 - \dfrac{(7 \times 12)^2}{(23)}$ $\dfrac{7 \times 12}{23}$	$= 12$
Below 1.4 Average	$5 - \dfrac{(9 \times 12)^2}{(23)}$ $\dfrac{9 \times 12}{23}$	$4 - \dfrac{(7 \times 12)^2}{(23)}$ $\dfrac{7 \times 12}{23}$	$2 - \dfrac{(7 \times 12)^2}{(23)}$ $\dfrac{7 \times 12}{23}$	$= 11$
N	9	7	7	$= 23$

Chi Square Result: 1.06 $p < .50 - .70$

E. Egotistical Scale

	Ramat Hakovesh	Sderot	Barbour	Total
Above 0.14 Average	$1 - \dfrac{(9 \times 2)^2}{(23)}$ $\dfrac{9 \times 2}{23}$	$0 - \dfrac{(7 \times 2)^2}{(23)}$ $\dfrac{7 \times 2}{23}$	$1 - \dfrac{(7 \times 2)^2}{(23)}$ $\dfrac{7 \times 2}{23}$	$= 2$
Below 0.14 Average	$8 - \dfrac{(9 \times 21)^2}{(23)}$ $\dfrac{9 \times 21}{23}$	$7 - \dfrac{(7 \times 21)^2}{(23)}$ $\dfrac{7 \times 21}{23}$	$6 - \dfrac{(7 \times 21)^2}{(23)}$ $\dfrac{7 \times 21}{23}$	$= 21$
N	9	7	7	$= 23$

Chi Square Result: 0.54

F. Zionist Scale

	Ramat Hakovesh	Sderot	Barbour	Total
Above 58 Average	$4 - (\dfrac{(8 \times 9)^2}{18})$ $\dfrac{9 \times 11}{18}$	$2 - (\dfrac{(6 \times 9)^2}{18})$ $\dfrac{6 \times 9}{18}$	$3 - (\dfrac{(4 \times 9)^2}{18})$ $\dfrac{4 \times 9}{18}$	= 9
Below 58 Average	$4 - (\dfrac{(8 \times 9)^2}{18})$ $\dfrac{8 \times 9}{18}$	$4 - (\dfrac{(6 \times 9)^2}{18})$ $\dfrac{6 \times 9}{18}$	$1 - (\dfrac{(4 \times 9)^2}{18})$ $\dfrac{4 \times 9}{18}$	= 9
N	8	6	4	= 18

Chi Square Result: 1.66 $p < .50 - .30$

TABLE A.6

Results on Behavioral Characteristic Categories

Ramat Hakovesh groups' scores denoted by x's for 1975 and o's for 1977 (only <u>madrichim</u> scoring included in these results). Mean Scores for 1977- 4.7 and for 1975 - 3.7. "5" represents the highest score and "1" the lowest score.

Categories	1	2	3	4	5
1. Outward Appearance				x	o
				o	x
				x	o
				x	o
				x	o
			x		o
				xo	
				x	o
2. Acceptance of Responsibility				xo	xo
				xo	xo
					xo
			x		o
			x	o	xo
			x	x	o
			x		xo
			x	x	o
	o	xo	x		o

3. Social Adjustment	xo		xo
	x		o
	x		o
		x	o
		x	o
		x	o
		x	o
		x	o
	x		
4. Social Position in the Group	x		o
	x		o
		x	o
		x	o
		x	o
		o	x
		x	o
			o
			o
5. Emotional Stability		x	o
		x	o
		x	o
		x	o
		x	o
		x	o
		x	o
		x	o
		x	o
6. Relationship to Work		x	o
		x	o
			xo
		x	o
		x	o
		x	o
		x	o
		x	o
		x	o

7. Relationship to Learning	1	2	3	4	5
				x	o
				x	o
				x	o
				x	o
				x	o
				x	o
			o	x	o
			x		o

8. Relationship to Authority of Madrichim and Others	1	2	3	4	5
		x	o		
	x	x	o		
	x		o		
		x	o		
		x	o		
		x	o		
			o		

9. The Ability to Control Oneself from Unbridled Impulses in Areas of Violence, Sexual Activity, and Taking Others Property	1	2	3	4	5
		x	o		
			x		
		x	o		
			x		
		x	o	x	
			o		
		x	o	o	
		x	o	o	

Sderot groups' scores denoted by x's (only carried out in 1977). Mean Score - 4.3. "5" represents the highest score and "1" the lowest score.

Categories	1	2	3	4	5
1. Outward Appearance				x	x
				x	x
				x	x
				x	x
2. Acceptance of Responsibility				x	x
				x	x
					x
				x	x

	1	2	3	4	5
3. Social Adjustment				x	x
					x
					x
			x	x	
			x		
4. Social Position in the Group					x
					x
					x
	x	x	x	x	
5. Emotional Stability	x	x	x	x	
			x	x	
				x	
6. Relationship to Work			x	x	
			x	x	x
			x		
			x		
7. Relationship to Learning			x	x	
			x	x	x
			x		
				x	x
8. Relationship to Authority of Madrichim and Others			x	x	x
			x	x	x
9. The Ability to Control Oneself from Unbridled Impulses in Areas of Violence, Sexual Activity, and Taking Others Property			x	x	x
				x	x
			x		
			x		

Barbour groups' scores denoted by x's (only carried out in 1977). Mean Score - 4.3. "5" represents the highest score and "1" the lowest score.

Categories	1	2	3	4	5
1. Outward Appearance				x	
				x	
				x	
				x	

2. Acceptance of Responsibility		x		
		x	x	x
				x
				x
3. Social Adjustment		x	x	x
		x	x	
		x		
		x		
		x		
4. Social Position		x		
	x			
	x			
	x			x
			x	
			x	
5. Emotional Stability				x
			x	x
			x	x
			x	x
6. Relationship to Work			x	
			x	
			x	x
			x	x
			x	
7. Relationship to Learning			x	
			x	
			x	
			x	
			x	
			x	x
8. Relationship to Authority of			x	x
Madrichim and Others	x		x	x
			x	
			x	

9. The Ability to Control Oneself from Unbridled Impulses in
   Areas of . . .

. . . Violence	x		x	x
		x	x	x
		x	x	x
. . . Sexual Activity		x	x	x
				x
				x
		x	x	x
. . . and Taking Others Property		x	x	x
			x	x
		x	x	x

Glossary of Hebrew Terms

Ashkenazim: Jews of European-American origin or Jews whose parents had lived in other English-speaking countries as: South Africa, Australia, and New Zealand. This group is also referred to as "Western."

Chevrat Noar: A term which refers to a peer group community of Israeli youth, aged thirteen to sixteen, which was absorbed in kibbutzim during the period after World War II. The members usually were from the same ethnic group(s) coming from Europe and North Africa en masse. The task of the chevrat noar was to help people tackle their emotional and social problems as individuals and develop coherent and self-disciplined groups.

Gadna: A troop of teenaged Israeli scouts.

Garin: A core or nucleus group of young people who represent the original seed group which settles in a kibbutz or other collective settlement. Many Israelis join a garin before the army service and settle in a kibbutz with it immediately after they finish their service.

Hachshara Hatzira: The two-year Youth Aliyah Program herein referred to as the Kibbutz Program or the Kibbutz Rehabilitation Program.

Kelet: Work framework for problem youth before entrance into the Kibbutz Rehabilitation Program. For boys, work was found in Israeli Army workshops; for girls, in nursery schools or beauty salons.

Kibbutz: (plural Kibbutzim): The Israeli collective settlements. In the context of this study, they were used to settle survivors of the Holocaust and absorb large numbers of North African and Middle Eastern Jewish youth after World War II, supplying a supportive and idealistic environment for problem youth.

Madrich (plural madrichim): A peer group model who directly supervises the chevrat noar on a day-to-day basis and guides the group through the various stages of its development by exerting authority as a charismatic type leader. He lives at the same settlement as the group does, usually as a member. A part-time madrich assists a group in its organizational work and activities once or twice a week. He is often paid by a youth movement or has volunteered his services during a pre- or post-army national service period. He may live in the city or be a kibbutz inhabitant who has moved to a town temporarily.

Metapelet (plural Metaplot): House mothers who are responsible for the administration of the household in a youth house for the kibbutz program. They serve as social models for the girls.

Nachal: The pioneering Israeli Army units' organization which set up or added to the manpower of kibbutzim under the auspicies of the Israeli Army, the Israeli youth movements, and the Jewish Agency.

Sepharadim: Jews whose origins were in North Africa, the Middle East, Greece, Turkey, Italy and the Iberian Penninsula. This group is also referred to as Eastern.

Yishuv: The area of Jewish settlement during the British Mandate period until 1947.

Youth Aliyah: The agency whose original task was to save Jewish youth from fascism in the 1930s but later extended its activities to rescuing and absorbing families in danger elsewhere in the world. In the context of this study, its activity of working with poor problem Jewish youth in Israel will be stressed.

Bibliography

ABC Evening News, August 31, 1991.

Aiken, Charlotte "Poverty Plus Violence." The Daily Oklahoman, April 23, 1991.

Cooper, Kenneth J. "Students Blaze Academic Trail Through
Summer's Dog Days." The Washington Post, July 11, 1991,
13.

CNN Newsnight Report, September 26, 1991.

Cummings, Judith "Black Crisis: Family Decline, Rising Poverty" Pittsburgh Press, December 7, 1983. 1.

Desmond and Smith "Rehabilitation, Counseling, and Delin-
quent Youth," The Forms, Methods, and Techniques of
Vocational and Educational Guidance, Ed. H. Hoxter,
Paris: UNESCO, 1984.

Deutsch, Karl The Nerves of Government. New York: The
Free Press, 1966.

Dobin, Louis "When Summer Camp Becomes a Sanctuary,"
Reform Judaism Magazine, New York: Union of American
Hebrew Congregations, Spring, 1991, pp. 36-37.

Frank, Ivan "Summary of the Questionnaire of the Camp
Program As It Was Perceived by Camp Staff Members."
Pittsburgh: July, 1975 (unpublished).

Hinton, Mick "Abandoned Teenagers Facing Bleak Christmas." The Daily Oklahoman, December 19, 1990, 5.

Honig, Sarah "To Close the Gap," Jerusalem Post Magazine, September 25, 1975, 5.

Hyman, Charles, and Louis Wright Encampment for Citizenship. Berkeley: University of California Press, 1962.

Jacob, Phillips, and Henry Teune The Integration of Political Communities. Phildelphia: L.B. Lippincott Co., 1964.

The Jerusalem Post, March 18, 1991, 6.

Killackey, Jim "One in Four Teens Consider Suicide, Study Says." The Daily Oklahoman, September 20, 1991, 1.

Kozol, Jonathan The Night Is Dark and I Am Far From Home. Boston: Houghton Mifflin, 1975.

Kushner, Rabbi Harold When Bad Things Happen To Good People. New York: Schocken, 1981.

Matshushima, John "Child Welfare Institutions for Child Care." Encyclopedia of Social Work I Ed. John Turner, National Association of Social Workers, 1977.

Millward, Robert Outdoor Education. University Park: Pennsylvania State University Press, 1970.

Myers, Nechemia "Delinquents in Khaki" The Jewish Chronicle of Pittsburgh. Pittsburgh, July 28, 1991.

Rinnot, Chanoch "Youth Aliyah" Immigration and Settlement. Tel Aviv: Keter Publishing House Ltd., 1973.

Ritter, Joseph "Youth Rehabilitation Program," A Report to the International Conference of Jewish Communal Service, Child Care Workshop. Tel Aviv, 1973.

Samuelson, Robert "Gibberish On Job Skills," The Washington Post July 11, 1991, A 15.

Ungar, Carol "Network Gives Teenagers Chance To Find A Home," The Jerusalem Post, July 24, 1987.

Weiner, Anita "Haifa University Study," Maon Notes. Jerusalem, Fall 1990.

Index

ABC, 74
Absorption, 17, 26, 29, 40
Abuse, 4, 6, 29, 30, 34, 83, 87
Acculturation, 37
Achievement, 35, 45, 46, 55, 57, 66, 88
Addiction, 16, 28, 35, 89, 99
Aiken, Charlotte, 6
Alcohol, 4, 6, 35
Amarillo, 29
Ashkenazim, 8
    see also "Western Jews"
Assimilation, 37, 40
At-risk, 1, 8, 12, 21, 34, 37, 77-79, 84

Barbour Center, 7, 8, 46, 50, 58, 60-71
Big Brothers, 34, 74
Boy's Ranch, 28-31

CBS, 34
Chevrat Noar (Youth Aliyah peer group), 42, 51
Cheyney College, 89, 90-94
CNN, 73

Cocaine, 86
Cohen, Justice Chaim, 38
Competency, 80, 81
Computer, 87, 90, 97
Connelley Skilled Trade Center, 23, 88
Cooper, Kenneth J., 35
Crime, 3, 4, 26, 34, 59, 73, 74, 90, 98f

Delinquency, 4, 6, 24, 27, 29, 32, 73
Desmond, Richard E., 4, 5
Detroit, 74
Deutsch, Karl, 12
Dobin, Louis, 1
Dropouts, 41, 81, 85
Duff's Business Institute, 16, 23, 85, 89-98
Dysfunctional, 4, 5, 17, 22, 35, 84, 100

Eastern Jews, 8, 9, 17, 21, 37-39, 49, 51, 57, 68, 69, 72, 76
Edmond, Oklahoma, 28, 29, 34
Eisenstadt, Shmuel, 9
Eitan, General Rafael, 9, 28
Encampment, 10, 11, 23, 42, 69
European Jews, 8, 39, 40, 50f

Failure, 4, 5, 15, 53, 73, 74, 98
Family-size, 79
Fenton, Bob, 32
Frank, Ivan, 24, 45

Gadna (Israeli paramilitary youth group), 18
Garin (Kibbutz core-group), 45-47, 52-60, 66-71
GED, 15
Government, 12, 21, 32, 35, 60, 75-82

Hachshara Hatzira (Youth training program), 1-3, 30, 50
Hadas, 1, 44, 45, 55, 57, 68
Harrisburg, 99
Highfields, 3, 16, 24, 27, 67, 102

High-risk, 1-5, 13, 17, 21-24, 34, 35, 67, 71, 75-78, 81-88, 91-96, 102
Hinton, Mick, 84
Homeless, 5, 16, 17, 30, 60, 102
Honig, Sarah, 9
Houseparents, 18, 30, 31-33, 45, 53
Hyman, Charles, 10, 11, 48

Ilich, Ivan, 10
Illiteracy, 9, 27
Integration, 1-3, 8-13, 19, 22-24, 30, 37-42, 48-54, 57-63, 66-72, 78, 101
IQ, 30

Jacob, Phillips, 11, 49
Jaffa, 46, 61, 70, 72
Jerusalem, 3, 9, 30, 33
Jewish Agency, 41
Job-developer, 90
Job-site, 89, 90, 93-95

Kelet (Youth Aliyah absorption program), 18, 29, 50, 56, 61, 64
Kfar Shalem, 46, 61
Kibbutz (Israeli agricultural collective), 1, 2, 17, 18, 22, 24, 26, 27, 29, 30, 34, 38-60, 63, 64, 67-71, 81, 101, 102
Killackey, Jim, 6
Klarman, Joseph, 41
Kozol, Jonathan, 2
Kushner, Rabbi Harold, 32

Landau, Justice Chaim, 38
Literacy, 9

Madrich (Counselor), 41-46, 51-69
Matshushima, John, 5
Mentors, 1, 74
Metapelet (House mother), 43, 45
Myers, Nechemia, 27, 28

Nachal (Pioneering Israeli Army units), 2, 18, 19, 42-47, 53-60, 65-71
Neighborhood, 7, 11, 27, 34, 35, 38, 45, 46, 53, 61, 69, 91

Oakland, 15, 16, 99
Oklahoman, 84
Orr Shalom, 3, 30-34

Parents, 5, 8, 30, 33-35, 40, 47, 49, 62, 64, 79, 83, 86
Peer, 10, 11, 22-29, 39-43, 48, 51-59, 66-71, 81, 83, 96, 101
Peer-tutoring, 80
Pittsburgh, 1-7, 15, 16, 22, 24, 67, 83-85, 89, 93, 96-99, 102
Poverty, 2, 5, 26, 29, 73, 74, 84, 97-99
Pregnancy, 93, 98

Race, 3, 11, 22, 29, 37, 83
Ramat Hakovesh, 1, 17-19, 41-47, 50, 53-72, 84, 102
RBI, 74
Residential, 5, 16, 22, 26, 27, 39-42, 47, 50, 62, 63, 66-70, 86, 93, 99-101
Rinnot, 40
Ritter, Joseph, 1, 17, 26, 52
Rogers, Robin, 1
Rostow, Walter, 10

Sabras, 8
Samuelson, Robert, 80, 81
Sderot, 41, 47, 57-66, 70, 71
Sepharadim, 8, 38, 53
    see also "Eastern Jews"
Sharon, Aaron, 1, 43, 46, 54, 70
Socialization, 17, 26, 27, 41, 42

Tel Aviv, 1, 2, 7, 8, 18, 26, 38, 41, 46-50, 53, 60, 61, 68, 70, 84
Teune, Henry, 11, 49
Tikvah Quarter, 18, 38, 46, 61
Tzahal (Israel Defense Force), 46

Unemployment, 5, 86, 95, 97-99

Volunteerism, 29, 33-35, 43, 75

Warehousing, 5, 15
Washington, DC, 22, 84
Weiner, Anita, 33
Welfare, 15, 40, 46, 50, 53, 66, 69, 71, 72, 77, 78, 101
Western Jews, 8-12, 22, 32, 34, 39, 40, 50, 56-59, 68, 70, 75, 99,
    101, 102
Wright, Louis, 10, 11, 48

Yishuv (Settlement), 39, 40
Yitzchak, 1, 43, 44, 54, 57-59, 68

Zionist, 39, 63, 64

About the Author

IVAN C. FRANK is Educational Director and Youth Director of the Jewish Community's Intercongregational Sunday School and Hebrew Schools of Emanuel Synagogue and Temple B'nai Israel in Oklahoma City. He lived with his family in a kibbutz from 1977 to 1982, during which time he was coordinator of the Education Department of the Regional College of the Negev and taught at Ben Gurion University. He worked with high-risk youth in Pittsburgh from 1982 to 1990 as a teacher, coordinator of an alternative educational program, psychometrist, and educational advocate.